200 SMALL APARTMENT IDEAS

200 SMALL APARTMENT IDEAS

Cristina Paredez Benítez

FIREFLY BOOKS

A FIREFLY BOOK

Published by Firefly Books Ltd. 2012

First printing

Publisher Cataloging-in-Publication Data (U.S.)

Benítez, Cristina Paredes.
    200 small apartment ideas / Cristina Paredes Benítez.
[800] p. : ill., col. photos. ; cm.
Includes index.
Summary: Various designs and interior decorations of apartments.
ISBN-13: 971-77085-045-3
1. Apartments. I. Two hundred small apartment ideas. II. Title.
747.88314 dc23   NK2195.A6B464 2012

Library and Archives Canada Cataloguing in Publication

Paredes, Cristina
    200 small apartment ideas / Cristina Paredes Benítez.
Includes index.
ISBN 978-1-77085-045-3
    1. Apartments. 2. Small rooms—Decoration.
3. Interior decoration. I. Title.
II. Title: Two hundred small apartment ideas.
NK2195.A6P37 2012   747'.88314   C2012-900981-4

Published in the United States by
Firefly Books (U.S.) Inc.
P.O. Box 1338, Ellicott Station
Buffalo, New York 14205

Published in Canada by
Firefly Books Ltd.
66 Leek Crescent
Richmond Hill, Ontario L4B 1H1

Cover design: Erin R. Holmes

Printed in China

This book was developed by:
LOFT Publications
Via Laietana, 32, 4°, of. 92
08003 Barcelona
Spain

Editorial Coordinator: Aitana Lleonart
Art Director: Mireia Casanovas Soley
Interior layout design: Claudia Martínez Alonso
Layout: Yolanda G. Román
English translation: Cillero & de Motta

Photo Credits
Front Cover: © Benjamin Boccas
Back Cover (From Left to Right):
© Andrei Margulescu, Parasite Studio
© .27 Architects
© Rien van Rijthoven
© Courtesy of Benjamin Boccas
© Michael Moran
© Pedro Martínez (fotoarquitectura.es)

INTRODUCTION

Paris, Buenos Aires, New York, Barcelona, Tokyo, Singapore... the one thing all of these cities have in common is high population densities. It is now a fact of life that high densities have resulted in lower availability of housing and higher prices. For this reason, the majority of city dwellers live in small apartments.

The layout and decor of an apartment requires thought and organization, even more so when the space is small. In these cases, consideration of needs and possible solutions must be more specific to be able to adapt to the available square footage. You must decide, for example, how to make best use of natural light, where to locate the bathroom, which space you dedicate to storage or whether it is convenient to combine rooms such as the dining room and the kitchen.

Some of the ideas are general and can be applied to all small apartments, such as how to create levels in double height spaces, increasing, as a result, the square footage, or how to use pale colors that visually amplify the rooms. But this book offers much more than the best-known solutions. It presents very diverse decorative styles and some original furniture solutions that serve as inspiration for a wide variety of tastes. This book attempts to prove that an apartment, no

matter how small, reflects the personality of the owner or the tenant, so you should by all means let your personality shine through. It is also very important that the apartment is equipped with all the spaces that you require.

This book is divided into five chapters that showcase ideas and solutions depending on the size of the apartment. The chapter XXS, for example, considers the "mini-apartment," up to 538 ft² (50 m²). The chapter XS covers homes up to 1,076 ft² (100 m²), and S those with less than 1,614 ft² (150 m²). Other chapters focus on topics that try to provide more solutions: renovation projects and blocks with small apartments. The fourth chapter provides ideas for homes that require remodeling (there are many of them), and offers very inspirational examples. The chapter dedicated to apartment blocks, normally excluded from this type of publication, shows how the initial design of an apartment block has an impact on the final layout of the interior spaces.

This journey through the exciting examples provides insight into the minds of architects who meet the needs of contemporary urban life with amenities like access to communal parking. Other contributions cover more sociological topics, such as bringing back a sense of community and creating open and shared spaces with neighbors.

XXS

TAMKA APARTMENT

Architect: **Jakub Szczęsny/Centrala**
Location: **Warsaw, Poland**
Photos: **Radek Wojnar**
Square footage: **231.5 ft² (21.5 m²)**

Although at first the project seemed unfeasible, this very small home of only 231.5 ft² (21.5 m²) includes all the distinct areas necessary for day-to-day living. The owner, a divorcé in his thirties, uses this centrally located apartment three or four times a week when he sees his son, and sometimes during weekends. There are three main pieces that make the most of the space: the raised bed, under which resides the washing machine and storage space, the shower next to the entrance and the moving wall that hides a small kitchen and becomes the dining room and work table.

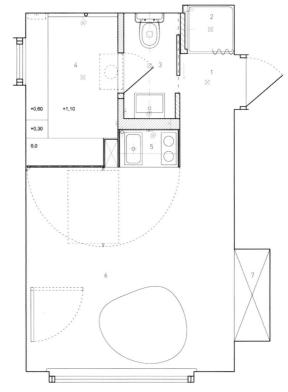

+0,60   +1,10

+0,30

0,0

Floor plan

1. Entrance
2. Shower
3. Bathroom
4. Bedroom
5. Kitchen
6. Living room
7. Built-in closet

The number one priority for this layout was maximum space for the living room area. For this reason, it does not matter that the shower is located next to the entrance hall and is plainly visible.

The idea of raising the bed to create extra storage space is perfect for small studios. The choice of colors, in this case purple and pistachio, defines the personality of the occupants.

1

2

Built-in cabinets and spaces provide valuable storage room, so they should be used as strategically as possible. In the bedroom, for example, the space under the bed has been used to install the washing machine.

RED NEST

Architect: **Paul Coudamy**
Location: **Paris, France**
Photos: **Courtesy of Benjamin Boccas**
Square footage: **247 ft² (23 m²)**

The challenge of fitting a bedroom, a bathroom, a study and a dressing area into a space of only 247 ft² (23 m²) forced Paul Coudamy to explore the possibilities of custom furniture to organize the areas. The undisputed central piece of this project is a mobile bookcase that when moved reveals the bed area and the study. The module manages to combine two spaces and increase the storage area without being visually overwhelming, and without affecting circulation through the area. The bathroom, a gray color that is completely different from the bright colors of the bedroom, is the most private corner in the apartment.

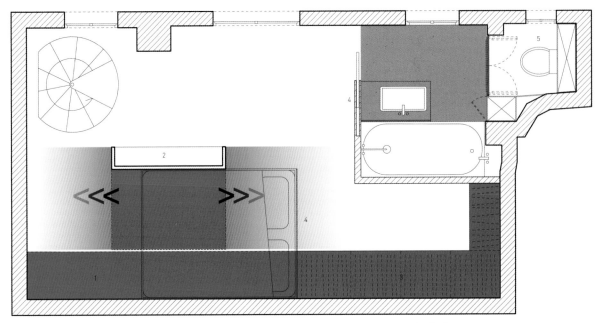

Floor plan

1. Desk
2. Mobile bookshelf
3. Dressing area
4. Stainless glass panel
5. Hidden washroom

The bed, study table and dressing area are located along one of the walls. In this way, two windows in the central space and a third in the bathroom are free to light up the space and enlarge it visually.

3

Besides being a functional room, the layout and the furniture avoid monotony. The access door to the space, a trapdoor in the floor, is another of the elements that gives this project an original flair.

The bright red lacquered furniture and matte white walls create a unique young, modern space. The lighting is created through natural light and custom fixtures in the furniture.

4

APARTMENT IN 3D

Architect: **Héctor Ruiz Velázquez**
Location: **Madrid, Spain**
Photos: **Pedro Martínez (fotoarquitectura.es)**
Square footage: **538 ft² (50 m²)**

This apartment, built in collaboration with ASCER (Spanish Association of Ceramics), is characterized by two elements: the use of ceramics as building material and the incredibly innovative distribution of space. The architect conceived this design with total freedom to use both horizontal and vertical space. There are no obstacles, and the ceramic tiles visually reinforce the area. The functions of the home (kitchen, bedroom, study and living room) are distributed over the different levels that have been created, thus achieving a better use of space and a dynamic distribution.

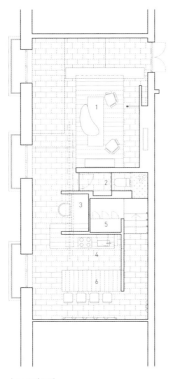

Lower level

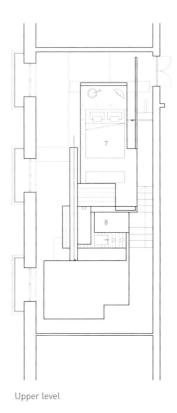

Upper level

1. Living room
2. Washroom
3. Study
4. Kitchen
5. Storage
6. Dining room
7. Bedroom
8. Bathroom

5

For the levels not to block the passage of natural light it is important to create openings, windows or gaps that allow light to pass through the different rooms. This solution also enables better spatial communication.

A solution for small spaces built with modules is to make use of the walls and other partitions to integrate shelves, cabinets or other storage spaces that allow the occupants to organize their belongings.

6

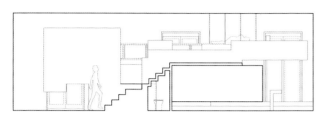

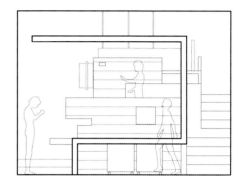

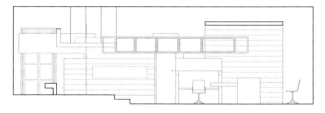

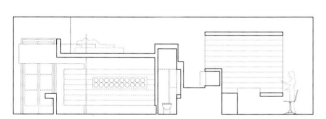

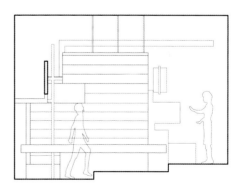

Longitudinal sections

Cross sections

The resistance of the materials chosen and their aesthetic strength may be the key to personal and original decor. The elongated shape of the ceramic tiles of the apartment reinforces the horizontal lines and visually enlarges the space.

7

The bedroom, located in the upper zone of the volume, is the most private area. The predominantly white color, the almost total lack of furniture and an original lamp create a magical atmosphere.

APARTMENT
IN CHAMBERÍ

Construction: **DEDENTRO**
Decoration: **Diana Díaz-Berrio Ibáñez**
Location: **Madrid, Spain**
Photos: **Germán Sainz, DEDENTRO**
Square footage: **538 ft^2 (50 m^2 + 50 m^2) terrace**

The owner of this apartment, Spain Select (www.spain-select.com), decided to completely renovate the interior to rent it. The decoration, therefore, should be timeless and welcoming to suit potential tenants. The new layout and custom furnishings made full use of every corner to create storage space and a feeling of spaciousness in only 538 ft^2 (50 m^2). The pale colors of the furniture and mirrors on the closet doors highlight the luminosity. The terrace has been renovated to add more surface area to the apartment and gain living space, especially in summer.

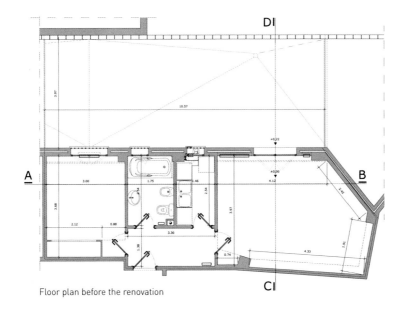

Floor plan before the renovation

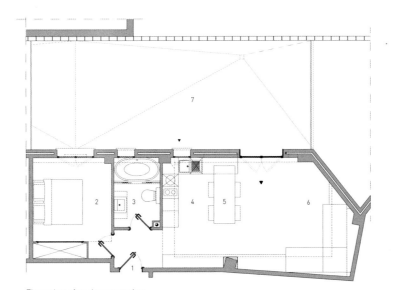

Floor plan after the renovation

1. Entrance
2. Bedroom
3. Bathroom
4. Kitchen
5. Dining room
6. Living room
7. Terrace

8   This small kitchen is integrated into the larger space with custom cabinetry in the same style and color as that found in the adjacent dining room.

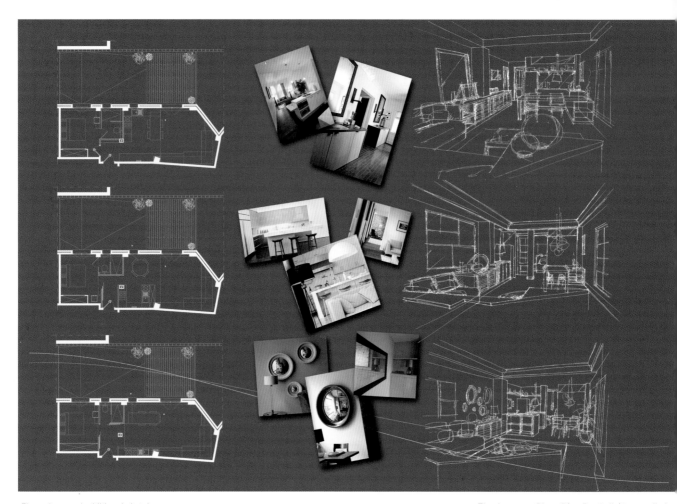

Floor plans and additional sketches

The decorator Diana Díaz-Berrio Ibáñez studied different spatial organizations before deciding on the final distribution. She also considered different decorative styles and finishes.

9 Use pale colors as base colors in small spaces. Hints of color that brighten the interior and define the aesthetics of the rooms can be achieved with small decorative objects.

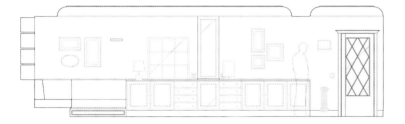
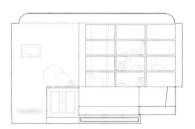

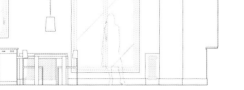
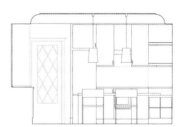

Interior elevations

Exterior spaces provide relief
to the occupants of small
apartments, although they
should not be considered in the
same way as an interior room.
Courtyards and terraces create
more space and promote new
uses and activities.

10

APARTMENT IN A VICTORIAN BUILDING

Designer: **Michelle Mason**
Location: **London, United Kingdom**
Photos: **Bill Osment**
Square footage: **527 ft² (49 m²)**

The owners of this apartment are the industrial designer Michelle Mason and her husband Bill, a photographer. She is responsible for the change that the apartment has undergone, a bright and welcoming space in an old Victorian style building. A small-scale renovation increased the size of the apartment, adding a bedroom to the attic. Furniture and other objects were not purchased specifically for the home, except for bathroom fittings. This shows that ideas and the imagination can be as, or more, important than good spatial design because creative solutions have to account for practical constraints.

11 The interior of the apartment boasts touches of bright colors such as turquoise or violet, but it is the color white that multiplies light and gives the space amplitude.

HOXTON
BARING STREET
HAMMERSMITH
HOXTON
SHOREDITCH
GREENWICH
PICCADILLY CIRCUS
BLOOMSBURY
Red Lion Square
ST PAULS
SLOANE SQUARE

MINILOFT

Architect: **Leone Design Studio**
Location: **Chelsea, New York, NY, USA**
Photos: **Steve Williams**
Square footage: **441 ft² (41 m²)**

The architects have managed to transform a tiny space into a bright and practical apartment. A lightweight staircase was designed to create the mezzanine floor where the bedroom is located. To avoid taking up too much surface and visually cluttering the interior, it was suspended from the ceiling by a series of wires that gives it lightness. The wood used in the steps, which is the same as that used in the kitchen, perfectly complements the oak floor covering. Both provide a warm counterpoint to an interior that also features the visual weight and toughness of stainless steel.

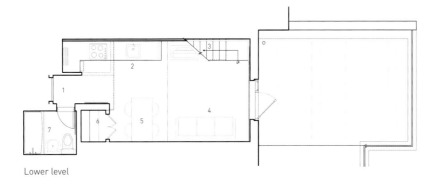

Lower level

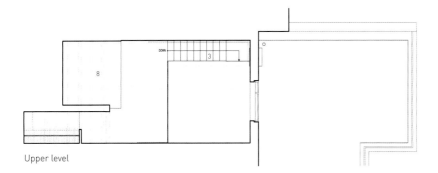

Upper level

1. Entrance
2. Kitchen
3. Stairs
4. Living room
5. Dining room
6. Closet
7. Bathroom
8. Bedroom

To avoid creating closed spaces and low ceilings, the mezzanines should not occupy the total surface area of the apartment. In this way, double-height spaces provide breadth.

12

13

Lighting in mezzanines is an important detail, even though the function of this room is secondary. The use of mid-height partitions or transparent materials avoids the excessive use of artificial lighting.

MR. CHOU'S APARTMENT

Architect: **CHRYSTALLINE Architect**
Location: **Jakarta, Indonesia**
Photos: **Courtesy of CHRYSTALLINE Architect**
Square footage: **484 ft² (45 m²)**

The size of the apartment demanded the optimization of each corner for organizing functions, the choice of the best materials, and the arrangement of the day to day activities. One of the most outstanding renovations was the change from traditional brick walls to a glass partition in the bathroom to increase the feeling of space. Privacy is ensured by sliding wooden panels. Another feature is the mirrored wall in the space that combines the living room, dining room and kitchen, which visually doubles the area of the apartment. The recessed lighting in the ceiling creates a relaxed and sober ambience.

In the dining area, different spaces and materials are combined. The sliding white oak plywood panels are mixed with custom white furniture and the maple floor, creating a flexible space.

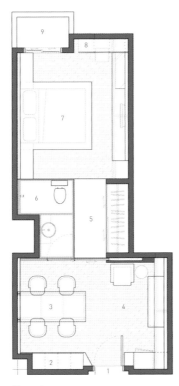

Floor plan

1. Entrance
2. Kitchen/laundry
3. Dining room
4. Living room
5. Closet
6. Bathroom
7. Bedroom
8. Work area
9. Balcony

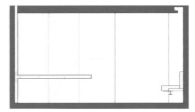

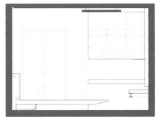

Sections

A good solution is to use intermediate spaces or hallways to position rooms or auxiliary elements. In this case, the bathroom and closet are located in a passageway that separates the two main spaces.

14

Everything in this apartment has been reduced to the minimum. The bathroom, enclosed by thin glass walls, contains a toilet, a sink and a small corner for the shower that goes virtually unnoticed.

ALUMINUM HOME

Architect: **Hideki Yoshimatsu/Archipro Architects**
Location: **Yokohama, Japan**
Photos: **Archipro Architects**
Square footage: **505 ft² (47 m²)**

This project was designed for a young married couple who wanted to live in the city center. The apartment was an old office, and the architects completely renovated the space to design the necessary areas of a home. A single space was devised, and the different areas were located around the perimeter. At one end is the kitchen, behind sliding panels. At the opposite end, there is a bookcase with translucent panels that, in addition to providing storage space, allows in natural light. The only enclosed space is the bathroom, where a few high windows provide natural light.

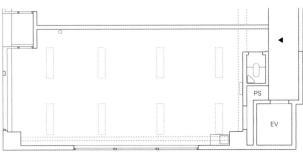

Floor plan before the renovation

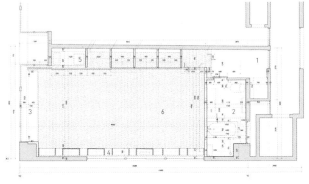

Floor plan after the renovation

1. Entrance   4. Shelving
2. Bathroom   5. Kitchen
3. Study   6. Bedroom

Regular-shaped surfaces allow
different applications to be
installed along the walls. In this
way, part of the space of each
room is shared and better use is
made of every square inch.

15

16

The study is next to the window that receives the most daylight. In the décor, prominent features include the ceiling, covered with aluminum slats, which provide an industrial touch to the interior and give the name to the project.

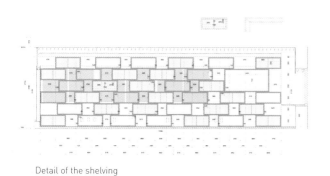

Detail of the shelving

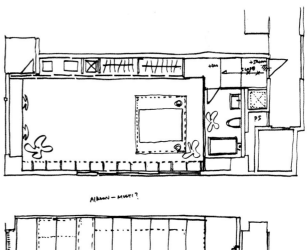

Sketches

GREEN DORMITORY PROTOTYPE

Architect: **Fabrica 718, Pratt Institute**
Location: **New York, NY, USA**
Photos: **Sean Hemmerle**
Square footage: **452 ft² (42 m²)**

The 1702 Living Lab project started in 2009 with the aim to sensitize students to sustainability in architectural design. Students and members of the Pratt Institute designed all the furniture and features of the space, a student dormitory, with the goal of reinventing, reusing, recycling and reducing. The materials, sustainable and locally sourced, were combined with LED lights and control systems for energy. This small apartment is a prototype to obtain information that can be used for future renovations of residence halls on campus.

Site plan of the building

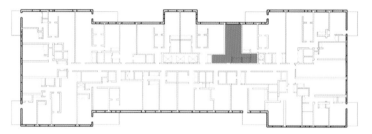

Site plan of the apartment

17

The furniture was conceived by the industrial design and interior design departments from the Pratt Institute. The goal of sustainability is evident in the choice of materials and manufacturing processes.

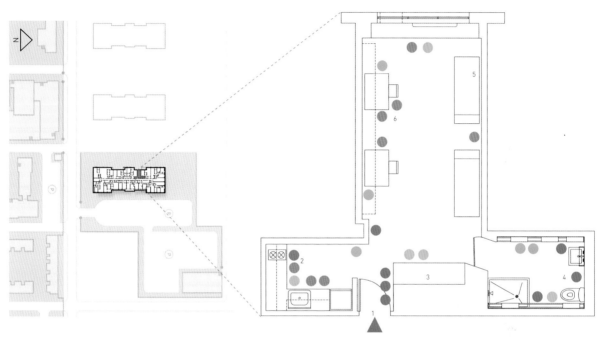

Floor plan

1. Entrance
2. Kitchen
3. Closet
4. Bathroom
5. Bedroom area
6. Study area

The red color of the floor plan shows the reused materials, and the blue elements reduce the electricity and water consumption. The orange indicates where the sustainable materials are and the yellow shows the elements designed at the Pratt Institute.

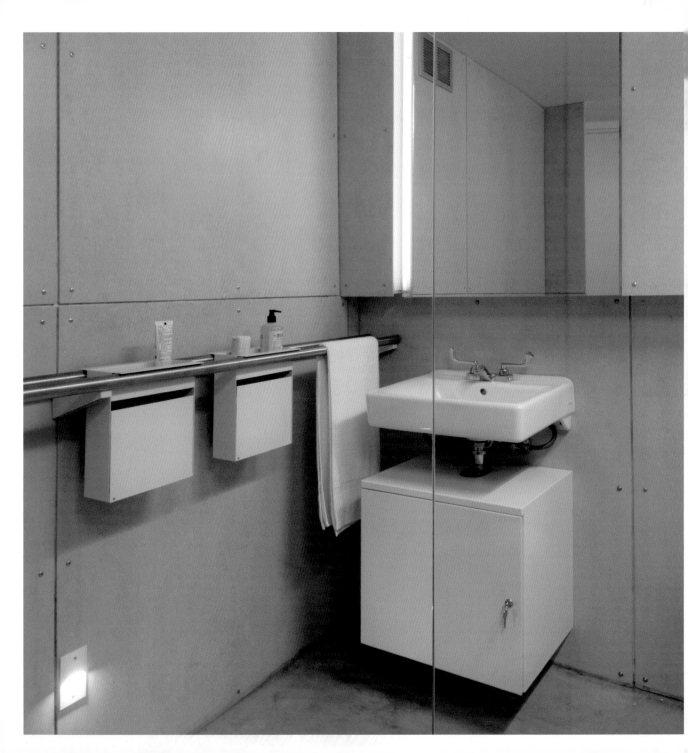

18   The objects designed by the
students and lecturers of the
Pratt Institute comply with two
equally important requirements:
to adapt to a small space and
respect sustainability criteria.

ADAPTED APARTMENT IN VIENNA

Architect: **S.DREI Architektur**
Location: **Vienna, Austria**
Photos: **Bernd Steinhuber**
Square footage: **430 ft² (40 m²)**

This renovation was a challenge for the architects, as they had to transform a small apartment with no bathroom into an apartment for two people that is fully accessible for wheelchairs. The first step was to install the elevator to reach the second floor. The objective was to install a bathroom without diminishing the already small size of the apartment. It was decided to remove a wall and install divider curtains. The layout and furniture were chosen to facilitate circulation through the apartment. The articulated bed and contemporary decor of the interior of the home stand out.

Instead of changing the location
of the wall that enclosed the
dining room, it was removed and a
curtain was put in its place. Width
and flexibility in the circulation
zones are very important in
adapted housing.

19

Floor plan

1. Entrance
2. Bathroom
3. Living room/dining room
4. Kitchen
5. Bedroom

20

For easy access, furnishings for adapted apartments are almost always low. This can present a challenge in selecting items such as kitchen cabinets.

The apartment did not have a bathroom, so a comfortable and functional space was designed from scratch. As it was an adapted home, the shower was fully integrated into the space. There is not even a curtain.

MY "MOBILE HOME"

Architect: **Paul Coudamy**
Location: **Paris, France**
Photos: **Courtesy of Benjamin Boccas**
Square footage: **301 ft² (28 m²)**

This apartment has been designed with mobile homes as inspiration, where space is fully exploited to meet the needs of the occupants. The kitchen and bathroom, relegated to one end of the apartment, leave a central space free to accommodate other functions: living room, dining room, guest bedroom, and so on. A peculiar red wall built with epoxy separates the main space from the bathroom, the only enclosed space in the entire apartment. The irregular shapes of this wall and the arrangement of the organic-style lights create a contrast with the straight lines of the custom-made furniture. This contrast avoids monotony.

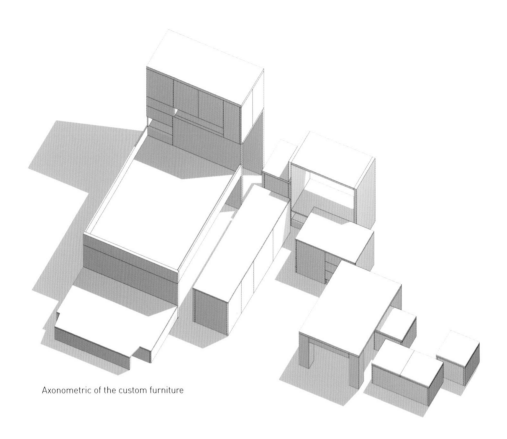

Axonometric of the custom furniture

The furniture, designed specifically for this
apartment, conceals a storage space, a table,
six seats, a bench and other places to store
clothes. The wheels located under the pieces
facilitate the transformation of the room.

21 The use of wood and different colors in the furniture and in different rooms of an apartment avoids visual monotony, especially in small apartments where several activities are carried out in one space.

HOME 08

Architect: **i29 | interior architects**
Location: **Amsterdam, The Netherlands**
Photos: **i29 | interior architects**
Square footage: **484 ft² (45 m²)**

The renovation of this small apartment has changed the layout of the rooms to maximize the space. The new plan distributes the functions into two units located in the walls. The entrance hall, a closet and part of the kitchen are concealed behind a pine wood wall. Beside it, another wall covered with wood includes a bench, a fireplace and more storage space. To prevent the wood from making the interior seem smaller, the floor, the ceiling and other walls have been painted white. The simplicity of the design makes this small space seem larger.

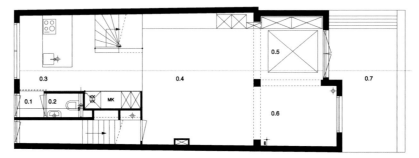

Floor plan

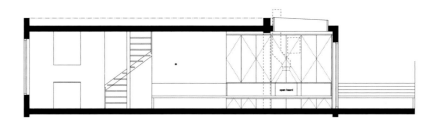

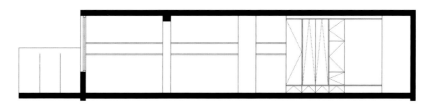

Sections

22   When it comes to designing
small apartments, you should
not overuse bold colors or eye-
catching textures, as they make
the spaces seem visually smaller.
The color white and wood are
mixed in correct proportion.

Not all apartments have large windows or glass expanses flooding the interior with natural light. Use white or other neutral or pale colors so that you are not left with dark corners.

23

MINILOFTS IN HELSINKI

Architect: **Pekka Littow Architectes**
Location: **Helsinki, Finland**
Photos: **Pekka Littow**
Square footage: **484 ft² (45 m²)**

The space under the roof of a Romantic style building in the Finnish capital has been used to accomodate two small homes. To create some contrast with the traditional architecture of the building, the interiors have been structured simply, with cubic compositions that accentuate the original walls. By creating a new interior within the old, the original objective was achieved: to build a timeless space. To free up space, bathrooms, kitchens and storage have been built as compact as possible and using a minimum range of materials and simple finishes.

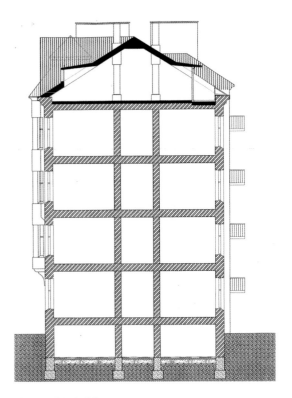

Section of the building

In some areas the walls were covered with cement mixed with transparent fixer, and in other areas the brick has been left exposed. The ceilings have been plastered in white, and the beams have been laminated in the same color to create a feeling of spaciousness.

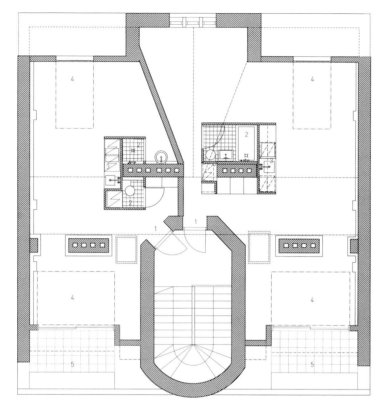

Floor plan

1. Entrance
2. Bathroom
3. Kitchen
4. Open space
5. Balcony

Compact or built-in furniture is desirable to save space. Several functions are combined in one leaving the rest of the apartment free for other functions.

24

LARCO APARTMENT

Architect: **Oneto/Sousa Arquitectura Interior**
Location: **Lima, Peru**
Photos: **Vinicius Barros**
Square footage: **506 ft² (47 m²)**

The interior design project of this contemporary apartment in Lima was carried out with the owner, who had a very clear idea of what he wanted for his home. The kitchen is located in a cube in the middle of the space and is the centerpiece of the lower level. One side is lined with white walls and another with dark wood paneling. As well as the kitchen, the living room, dining room and powder room are on this level. The high ceilings and discretion in the furniture make for a spacious ambience, and the presence of the color white and concrete creates a contemporary and modern aesthetic.

The double height of the apartment adds more space, as the bedroom and main bathroom are located on the top floor, which has remained half-open and connected to the lower level. This also increases the natural light.

25

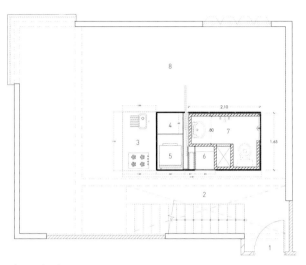

Lower level

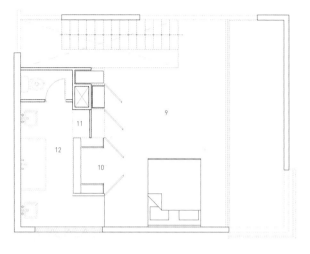

Upper level

1. Entrance
2. Stairs
3. Kitchen
4. Cupboard
5. Refrigerator
6. Ovens
7. Guest bathroom
8. Living room/dining room
9. Bedroom
10. Closets
11. Washing machine
12. Bathroom

This kitchen is not laid out in a traditional
style. It is fully integrated into the space.
To use the different components, the
owner has to move around the cube.

BORN DISTRICT LOFT

Architect: **Barbara Appolloni**
Location: **Barcelona, Spain**
Photos: **Christian Schallert**
Square footage: **237 ft² + 301 ft² (22 m² + 28 m²)**

This small apartment in the cosmopolitan district of Born in Barcelona stands out for the flexibility of its spaces and the ability of the architect to turn such a small area into a livable space with character. The rooms are superimposed, as it were, through the clever distribution of furniture and spaces: bedroom, study, kitchen, etc. The renovation reaches the terrace, on two levels, which increases the livable area of the home, especially in summer. Cement particle board and plywood, which conceal the furniture in each area, such as the kitchen, bathroom and closet, are used as interior materials.

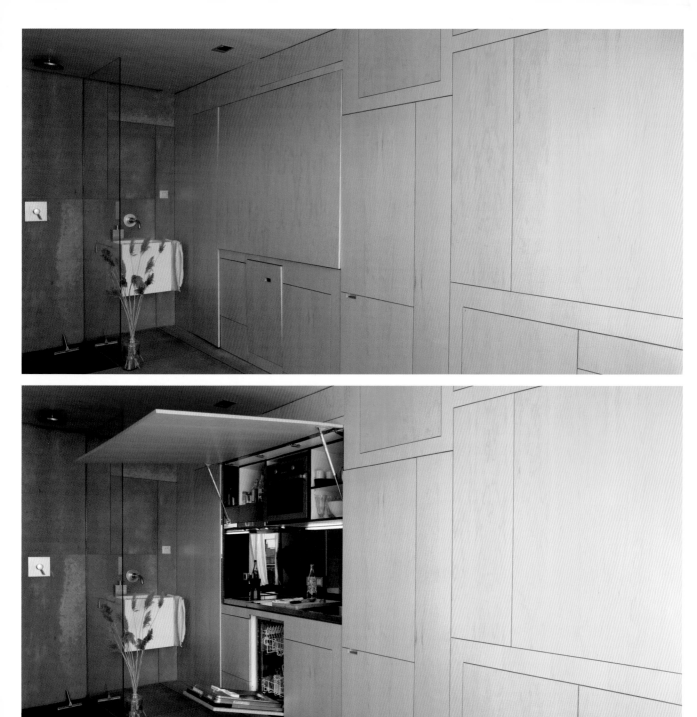

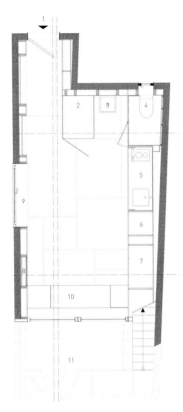

Apartment floor plan

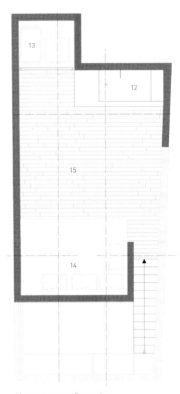

Upper terrace floor plan

The floor plans display the flexibility of this small space and how the different uses (kitchen, dining room, dressing room, bedroom, laundry room, exterior living area, etc.) have been positioned around the central areas of the living space and the terrace.

26

1. Entrance
2. Shower
3. Sink
4. Separate toilet
5. Kitchen
6. Refrigerator
7. Closet
8. Folding table
9. Folding shelf
10. Sofa bed
11. Terrace 1
12. Outdoor bathtub
13. Laundry
14. Lounge
15. Terrace 2

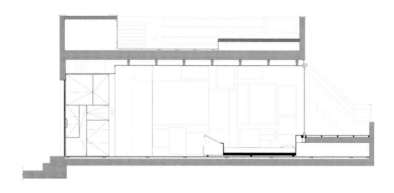

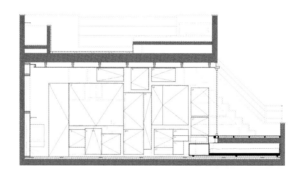

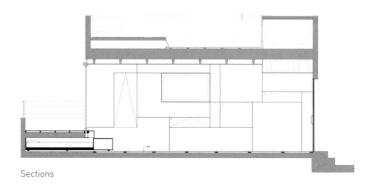

Sections

A combination of pieces creates different
rooms. For example, the bed, which is housed
under the terrace, serves as a sofa when it
is hidden. A couple of cement particle board
shelves unfold to form a study or dining room.

27 City terraces in temperate climates increase the living area of apartments, as they can be used almost all year long. The first terrace is an outdoor dining area, and on the second terrace is the laundry room, lounge and a bathtub.

XXS
FURNITURE

29

Irregular floor plans in apartments allow for original solutions. The bed in this small studio is concealed to allow more free space in the central area during the day.

28

In this bedroom, a piece of furniture containing the structure of the bed, a desk, and a chair saves space and creates visual continuity.

Jaco D. de Visser, Odette Ex
© Oliver Shuh/Palladium Photodesign

30

Custom furniture makes use of spaces that might not be utilized, such as those beneath the roof. One example is the solution found in this apartment for the beds and closets in the nursery.

31

An ottoman bed is one of the clearest examples of how furniture can transform and help to organize a home. The transformation might not always be evident, as in this case, with the bed concealing a small storage unit.

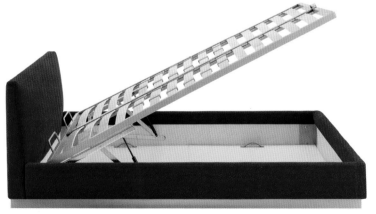

Zanotta © Zanotta

33

It is not necessary to have certain rooms if you do not have the space for them. Convertible furniture can give one room several functions at different times of the day.

32

The secret to great custom furniture that provides solutions that best suit each case, is to reflect upon the needs of each family. During the day, the bedroom becomes a study thanks to a movable wall.

34

Custom design must change the usual concept of interiors: it is not the owner who should adapt to the space, but the space that should accommodate the needs of the owner.

36

In small areas, custom furniture should not block the entry of natural light, which creates amplitude in the interior. A cabinet under the window, for example, provides storage space without interfering with the lighting.

35

Convertible furniture must consider the owners' lifestyle so that it allows the simultaneous use of some areas, such as the kitchen and the dining room or the bedroom and the bathroom.

37

The installation of closets and storage spaces should not be left to the last moment in interior design, as it may interfere with the layout of the rooms. A linear closet is suitable for wide hallways.

XS

CANALE APARTMENT

Design: **Kimberly + John Canale**
Location: **New York, NY, USA**
Photos: **Jen Huang**
Square footage: **650 ft² (60 m²)**

The owners of this small duplex in Brooklyn, who became parents in 2011, spent the summer of 2009 designing and implementing changes to transform this space into their new home. The kitchen, the dining room, the living room and a washroom are on the lower level. The bedrooms and the main bathroom are on the upper level. The apartment has a terrace with magnificent views of the neighborhood and the Statue of Liberty. The kitchen and the bedroom closets were bought from IKEA, not only because of their good value for money and style, but because the storage options adapted to the needs of the new family.

The owner, founder of a graphic design company, has a small workspace that does not lack any detail. A perforated panel is the perfect solution to have everything at hand.

38

Family keepsakes and collections purchased
in markets here and there are displayed
around the home. Their positions are
changed with other objects throughout
the year to create different ambiences.

The decorative objects of an apartment are a sample of the personality and tastes of the owners. An old metal box and a custom lamp make this apartment unique and singular.

39

PISTONS

Architect: **MAAJ Architectes**
Location: **Paris, France**
Photos: **Marc-Antoine Richard**
Square footage: **764 ft² (71 m²)**

This Parisian duplex project was done with the aim to respect the small dimensions of the space but give it functionality. The first solution was to give the architectural features dual functions. The second, but no less important solution, was to increase the amount of light that entered the home. The renovation maximized the diffused light that was obtained through the east-west orientation. In practice, natural light enhances the feeling of spaciousness and completely transforms the interior. The height of the ceilings allowed for a mezzanine floor where the bedrooms are located.

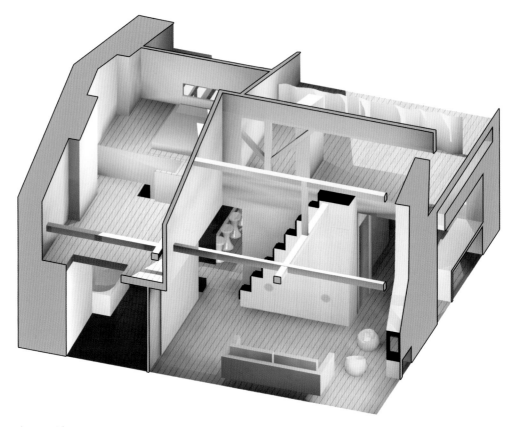

Axonometrics

The diagram shows one of the staircases in the apartment. This is a major element in the apartment, combining the structural function of connecting levels with the function of storage.

40

Natural light is almost indispensable in small spaces. It is important to never impede its passage throughout a space, and to make the most of elements that allow its entry such as windows and skylights.

41

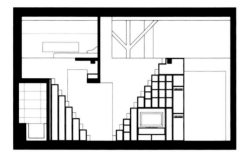

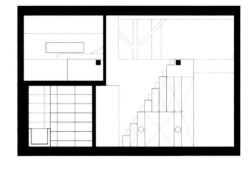

Sections

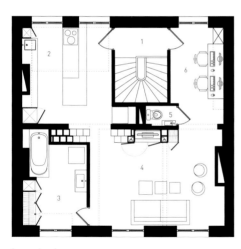

Lower level

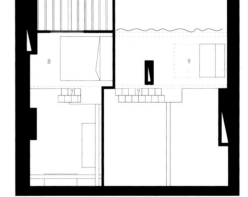

Upper level

1. Entrance
2. Kitchen
3. Bathroom
4. Living room
5. Washroom

6. Study
7. Staircase
8. Master bedroom
9. Guest bedroom

M+17

Architect: **Aurora Polo/Pensando en Blanco**
Location: **Hondarribia, Spain**
Photos: **Borja Garmendia**
Square footage: **990 ft² (92 m²)**

The renovation in this attic led to the recovery of the original structure of wooden beams, and redistributed the rooms in a more efficient way and more consistent with the style of living. The home is organized into several rooms separated into daytime and nighttime areas: living/dining room, kitchen, terrace, washroom, study, bedroom and bathroom. A terrace completes this apartment with views overlooking the old part of town. The day area faces East to make better use of sunlight. The private area is situated in the attic, which is naturally warmer, and the location of which benefits from great views of the sunset.

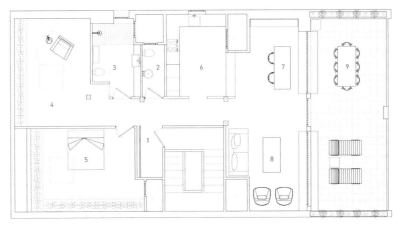

Floor plan

1. Entrance
2. Bathroom
3. Ensuite bathroom
4. Study
5. Bedroom
6. Kitchen
7. Dining room
8. Living room
9. Terrace

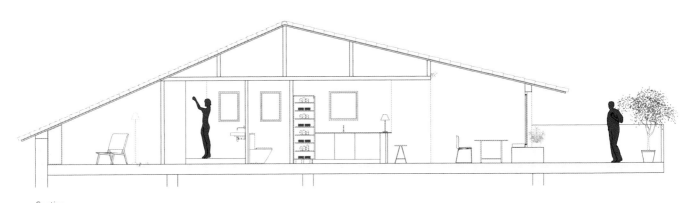

Section

42

In areas with unique dimensions,
such as attics, it is often easier
to have furniture and cabinetry
made to measure. The installation
of stock elements can mean that
the space is not used properly.

43

The interior layout and
large windows that govern the
two façades of the dwelling
guarantee natural ventilation
and abundant light in all spaces.
The large terrace provides
additional space.

ILLUSTRATOR'S APARTMENT

Designer: **Tad & Jessica Carpenter**
Location: **Kansas City, MO, USA**
Photos: **Eric Linebarger/LimenLime Photography**
Square footage: **1,165 ft² (108 m²)**

This apartment, located in a building from the early 20th century, was the bachelor pad of an illustrator and designer, Tad Carpenter, but was renovated to start a new life with his wife Jessica. The spaces are interconnected, and the majority of the partitions have been designed with walls that are open at the top or with shelves, which visually makes the space seem larger. The couple loves the combination of vintage aesthetics mixed with other more contemporary elements. The old signs and posters, the typographic pieces and children's books all stand out, giving the home a relaxed and cheerful aspect.

Maximum use of the kitchen area should be made when there is not much space. One of the most common solutions is to install a work island. In this case, the island has some supplementary shelves that can be spread out when necessary.

44

Storage furniture can bring personality to a home, especially if it is mixed with other styles. The brick walls and the white furniture unit that stores paper create an interesting industrial aesthetic.

45

The antique furniture and decorative objects create a cozy and charming ambience. In this home, for example, the collection of vintage globes and framed posters of old comics are prominent features.

46

The bedroom is one of the few rooms closed to the rest of the apartment and it has a much simpler aesthetic. Typography is also a theme, evident in the large golden C hanging over the bed.

CUBBY HOME

Architect: **Edwards Moore**
Location: **Melbourne, Australia**
Photos: **Peter Bennetts**
Square footage: **760 ft² (70.6 m²)**

The renovation of this apartment had to add useful floor space, and took advantage of the height of the ceilings to build an elevated level to position the private rooms and expand the apartment to 760 ft² (70.6 m²). The custom-designed furniture made from particle board panels is one of the most prominent elements, and personalizes the interior and makes it unique. The lower level contains the entrance area, with a closet of gold mirror-style doors, a separate toilet, the kitchen, the living room and a dining table. The upper level, accessed by an original white staircase, is home to the bedroom and bathroom area.

Lower level

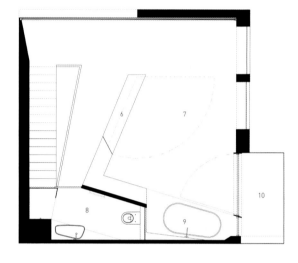

Upper level

1. Mirror-style wardrobes
2. Living room
3. Balcony
4. Separate toilet
5. Kitchen

6. Pivoting cabinet
7. Bedroom
8. Washroom
9. Bath
10. Courtyard

The choice of materials can completely change the aesthetics of an apartment. If you combine warm materials, such as wood, with cold materials, such as concrete or metal, it must be done carefully to achieve a balance.

47

48

The skylights in the roof and glass handrail turn the staircase area into a bright and cheerful circulation area. The mirror-style doors reflect more light and further enlarge the space.

49 The use of low cost materials, such as the particle board panels that form the headboard and the furniture surrounding the bed, achieves a great effect without a large budget.

OLD PEAK ROAD

Architect: **Ptang Studio**
Location: **Hong Kong, China**
Photos: **Ulso Tsang**
Square footage: **1,001 ft² (93 m²)**

The owner of this apartment, who spends much of the year traveling, did not need too much storage space, so the architects had more freedom to design the new apartment. "Natural" and "green" concepts have been used as the main theme of the renovation, and are present in the decoration of the entire apartment. The result of the renovation is a clear and bright space. The most remarkable piece in this regard has been the replacement of the study's partition wall with a glass wall, which blurs the boundaries between the rooms and integrates but does not combine the study with the rest of the apartment.

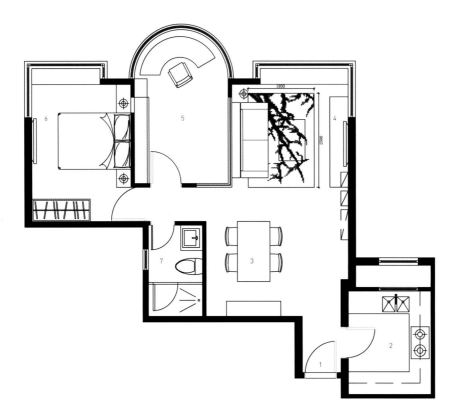

Floor plan

1. Entrance
2. Kitchen
3. Dining room
4. Living room
5. Study
6. Bedroom
7. Bathroom

It is advisable to position the most used spaces in well lit areas, to enjoy the natural light and reduce electricity consumption. In this case, the study, the living room and the bedroom are the chosen rooms.

50

The color white is the protagonist of the interior. To avoid an overly cold and austere style, the monochrome is broken with small decorative objects in shades of green, which also provide a more youthful and cheerful air to the interior.

51

In the bedroom, natural motifs match those found elsewhere in the apartment. The closet doors, for example, feature plant patterns in relief.

APARTMENT IN TOKYO

Architect: **Naoto Mitsumoto, Naoko Hamana/mihadesign**
Location: **Tokyo, Japan**
Photos: **Sadao Hotta**
Square footage: **769 ft² (71.5 m²)**

This apartment in Tokyo has undergone a renovation that has completely transformed it. The original space, a one-bedroom apartment with a room for the tea ceremony, had to be adapted for a family of five members. The completely radical change had to be carried out in an area of 769 ft² (71.5 m²). The solution was to design and build two modules, the wooden box and the blue box, in which the bedrooms are housed, creating an apartment and a half in a single space. A play area and a study have been created for the children. Neither of these two new modules reaches the ceiling, which avoids visually closing the space.

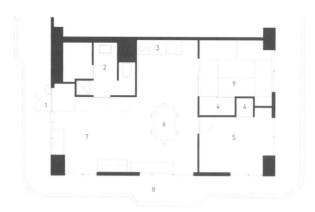

Floor plan before the renovation

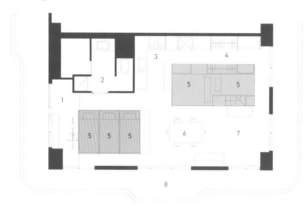

1. Entrance
2. Bathroom
3. Kitchen
4. Closet
5. Bedroom
6. Dining room
7. Living room
8. Balcony
9. Tea ceremony room

Floor plan after the renovation

The needs of a family define the layout required in a home. In this case, a completely different organization of space makes the most of the common rooms and reduces the square footage of the bedrooms.

52

The custom furniture adapts
to the individual needs. In this
apartment, each of the mini-
bedrooms has a small space for
books and toys.

53

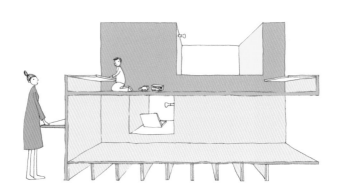

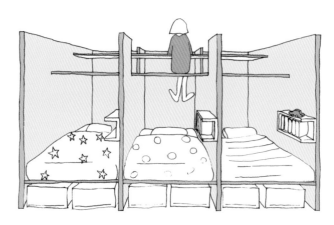

Sketches

As well as being useful and functional, these boxes are unique spaces. Comfort has been fused with a modern aesthetic and simple lines to be even more effective.

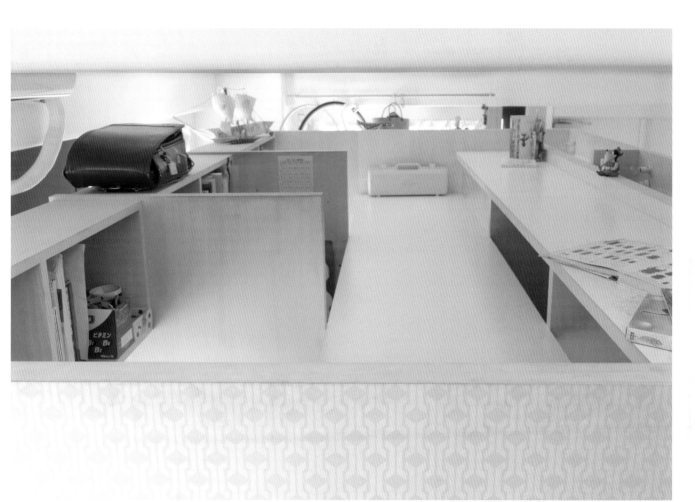

54

If there is enough height, an additional attic or mezzanine may be created, either to increase the storage area or the number of rooms.

CZERWENKA FOUNDATION APARTMENT

Architect: **Susanne Zottl/Zottl Buda, Kristof Jarder**
Location: **Vienna, Austria**
Photos: **Mario Buda, Loxpix**
Surface area: **1,076 ft² (100 m²)**

The former apartment of opera singer Oskar Czerwenka (1924–2000), located in the center of Vienna, was renovated and adapted for the rental market. The presence of a central body of sculptural forms gives personality to the home. The aim of this structure, which also houses the storage space, was to welcome residents and visitors and connect the living room with the kitchen and dining area, as well as improve the lighting. Also, its shape provides privacy to the bathroom and bedroom.

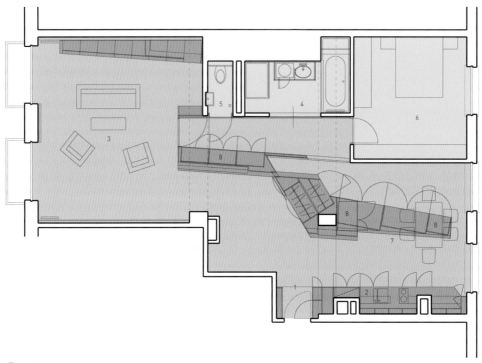

Floor plan

The shape of the sculptural module is
original and gives the interior a strong
personality despite the austerity that has
been used to choose colors and materials.

1. Entrance
2. Kitchen
3. Living room
4. Bathroom
5. Separate toilet
6. Bedroom
7. Dining room
8. Storage

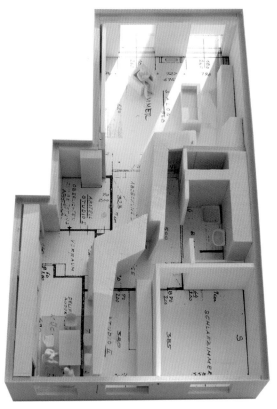

Models

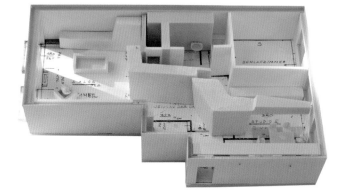

55

Lighting must be carefully planned in small spaces for functionality and aesthetics. Part of the lighting has been installed in the module, recessed into some of its gaps, which accentuates the theatrical aspect of the structure.

The structure and the shape of the furniture can define the ambience of an apartment. The orientation of the module in the apartment, located diagonally, brings dynamism to the interior, resulting in a unique, modern take on housing.

56

ATTIC IN COPENHAGEN (1)

Architect: **Norm Architects**
Location: **Copenhagen, Denmark**
Photos: **Jonas Bjerre-Poulsen**
Square footage: **904 ft² (84 m²)**

The client's desire was to achieve a completely minimalist apartment and take advantage of the city views. To achieve these objectives, a comprehensive renovation was carried out. Several partition walls were removed to reinforce the idea of spaciousness and make the high ceilings stand out. The colors used, white and black, are reminiscent of a minimalist style and create an almost monastic aesthetic. To unify the style of the single space, a white synthetic resin floor was used and the central space was painted matte black. Another important part of the renovation was removing details such as knobs and accessories.

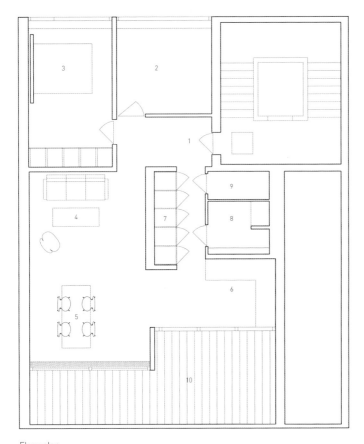

Floor plan

1. Entrance
2. Guest bedroom
3. Master bedroom
4. Living room
5. Dining room
6. Kitchen
7. Closet
8. Bathroom
9. Storage
10. Terrace

Using the same flooring throughout the apartment helps to unify the style and, in the case of small apartments, it creates a spatial continuity that helps to make the rooms appear larger.

57

For a minimalist interior, the furniture should be chosen carefully. In this apartment the TV has been integrated into the dark wall, and the white kitchen cabinets without handles are mixed with the walls of the space.

58

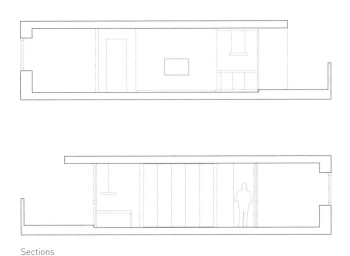

Sections

Indirect lighting has been installed under the main body of the apartment. The structure appears to float and manages to bring lightness to the space.

MODEL HOME

Architect: **CJ Studio**
Location: **Taipei, Taiwan**
Photos: **Marc Gerritsen**
Square footage: **1,097 ft² (100 m²)**

The interior design of this apartment has focused on the distribution of spaces. With changes in the organization and the location of the rooms, you can achieve more consistent uses that are tailored to the needs of the occupants, resulting in better use of space. The use of different floor coverings in this home divides the apartment into an area containing the kitchen, a bathroom, a study and a bedroom, and another area that combines the living room, the dining room and the master bedroom. These two areas, however, have no physical separation, so they are perceived as a large single space.

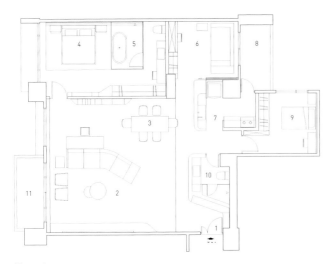

Floor plan

1. Entrance
2. Living room
3. Dining room
4. Master bedroom
5. Master bathroom
6. Study/guest bedroom
7. Kitchen
8. Laundry
9. Bedroom
10. Bathroom
11. Balcony

Besides the visual separation of space thanks to the floor covering, this apartment stands out because of the curved lines of the furniture, which add a softer touch to an environment dominated by sober colors.

59 If the room is big enough, a small
side table behind the sofa can
serve as a room divider.

It is advisable to fit curtains,
blinds or shades to adjust the
amount of light entering a room.
Even in small spaces, if you
choose the right material and
form, these elements will not
dwarf the rooms.

60

61

A good way to establish separate zones without building partitions is to use different types of floor covering. Alternatively, you can also the same material but in a different color or arrangement.

ATTIC IN COPENHAGEN (2)

Architect: **Norm Architects**
Location: **Copenhagen, Denmark**
Photos: **Jonas Bjerre-Poulsen**
Square footage: **796 ft² (74 m²)**

The basic design idea of this apartment was to create a calm and peaceful space for the owners, a Danish couple, who, although they live in Spain, travel a lot. The structures and the original floor were maintained, and these elements were used to create niches in which to install hidden lights. This lighting produces a clear, light and simple interior that generates cozy spaces. The home automation control system allows the owners, with just a touch on their iPhone, to control the heating, the air conditioning and the lighting of the apartment as soon as they get off the plane.

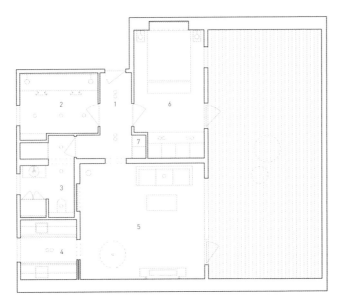

Floor plan

1. Entrance
2. Study
3. Bathroom
4. Kitchen
5. Living room
6. Bedroom
7. Closet

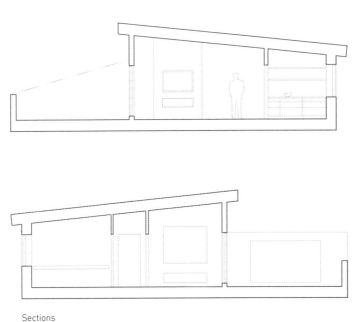

Sections

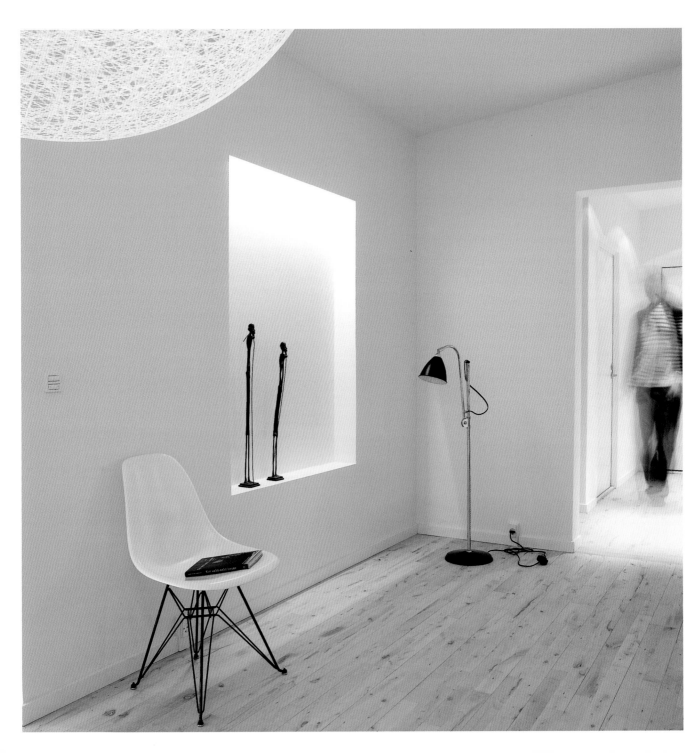

62   The built-in cabinets and mirrors are two simple solutions to maximize space. Mirrors, in addition to visually doubling the space, increase the illumination of the area.

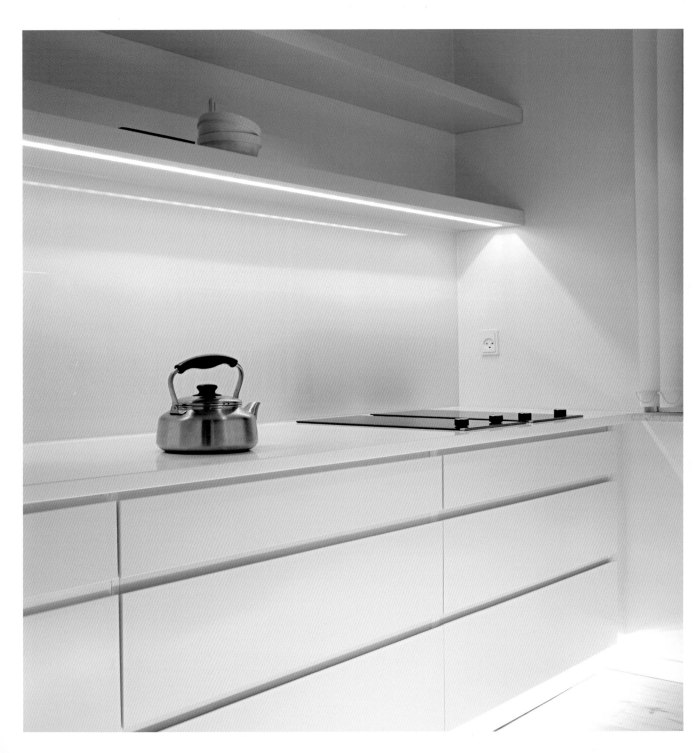

63 To achieve open spaces, use smooth surfaces and light colors that reflect the light better. In this case, the recessed lights give off a warm light that is dispersed throughout the bedroom.

The bathroom lighting, recessed into the ceiling and behind the mirror, creates a theatrical and sophisticated atmosphere. Although straight lines prevail throughout the apartment, the circular travertine sink in the bathroom softens the appearance.

JEHONA

Architect: **Vehap Shehi/VSA concept**
Location: **Brussels, Belgium**
Photos: **Vehap Shehi**
Square footage: **592 ft² (55 m²)**

This apartment is located very near the center of the city, in a typical Brussels-style construction. The dimensions of the home 592 ft² (55 m²) and the desire for a spacious area forced the architect to open spaces as much as possible. It was finally decided to pull down the wall separating two rooms and create a unique space where the kitchen, the dining room and the living room were located. In addition, an integrated wall unit was built that left a free space on the floor to place a sofa. In the bedroom, the bathroom and the closet were installed along one of the walls to achieve breadth and unify the decor.

64   Custom furniture is one of the
solutions that best fits small
spaces. It makes use of the
smallest corner and adapts
perfectly to the aesthetics sought
by the owners.

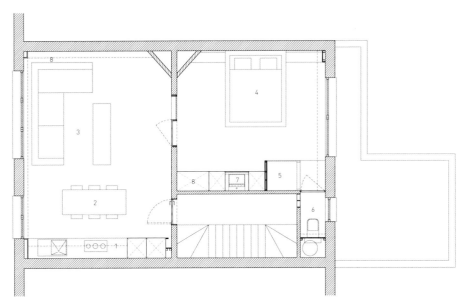

Floor plan

1. Kitchen
2. Dining room
3. Living room
4. Bedroom
5. Shower
6. Separate toilet
7. Sink
8. Storage

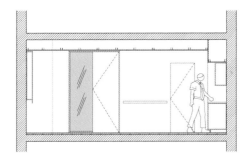

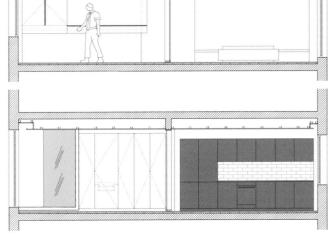

Sections

The oak floor of the bedroom was chosen to contrast with the clean, straight lines that dominate the rest of the apartment, which is a mixture of white, black and variations of gray.

If you want a minimalist
environment, conceal some
spaces behind cabinet doors or
flat panels. In this case, the sink
is concealed behind the cabinet
doors, and the separate toilet
behind a gray panel next to the
shower.

65

ADAPTED APARTMENT
IN INNSBRUCK

Architect: **S.DREI Architektur**
Location: **Innsbruck, Austria**
Photos: **Angelo Kaunat**
Square footage: **968 ft² (90 m²)**

The changes an apartment must undergo to adapt to people in wheelchairs are not incompatible with the good organization of space. This home and previous examples show that, even in a small space, good architecture and affordability are perfectly compatible. The hallways and doors of this home were enlarged to meet the needs of the family. The height of the toilets was lowered and the kitchen units were modified. The biggest challenge, however, was to ensure access to the balcony, a problem that was solved with an electric ramp.

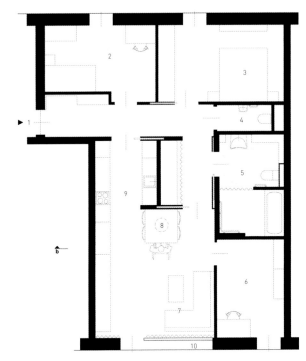

Floor plan

1. Entrance
2. Children's bedroom
3. Master bedroom
4. Washroom
5. Bathroom
6. Study
7. Living room
8. Dining room
9. Kitchen
10. Balcony

The floor plan of this apartment is not much different from a conventional apartment. In this case, the width of corridors and door knobs that do not stick out too far are the prominent features.

Open, wide spaces are a goal, not only in adapted housing, but also in small apartments. Clear space allows for better circulation and a better perception of the rooms.

66

JOCS FLORALS APARTMENT

Architect: **Vora Arquitectura**
Location: **Badalona, Spain**
Photos: **Adrià Goula**
Square footage: **753 ft² (70 m²)**

This three-bedroom apartment and terrace was originally dominated by a diagonal wall and a poor distribution of public and private spaces. The new layout streamlines these spaces: now the bedrooms are together and the living room is next to the terrace. The new plan also improves the lighting and circulation around the apartment. The common areas are based on the concept of "full" and "empty:" the living room, the hall and the hall area are the empty spaces, the bedrooms, the bathroom and the kitchen are the filled spaces. This conceptual division is based on the use of color: white for daytime areas and colors for the service areas and the private rooms.

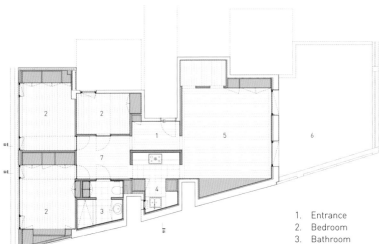

Floor plan

1. Entrance   5. Living room
2. Bedroom   6. Terrace
3. Bathroom   7. Hall
4. Kitchen

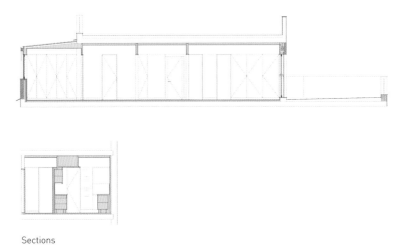

Sections

67   The new hall helps to streamline the circulation in the home. These small areas are essential to organize spaces, but should avoid taking up too much floor space, especially in small apartments.

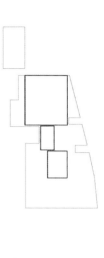

Conceptual diagrams

BADALONA SPACE

Architect: **Entre 4 Parets**
Location: **Badalona, Spain**
Photos: **Sandra Pereznieto**
Square footage: **1,022 ft² (95 m²)**

This attic was renovated to accommodate the needs of new occupants. The main idea was to design an apartment with open spaces as the central pieces, and as a link between the daytime and nighttime areas. This was to be as lightweight as possible to get the most out of the available floor space. The renovation creates a contrast between the old layout, a hallway with many setbacks and several elements that divide up the space, and the new distribution, a single corridor with built-in closets. The lightness of the space is reinforced by the use of austere materials and colors.

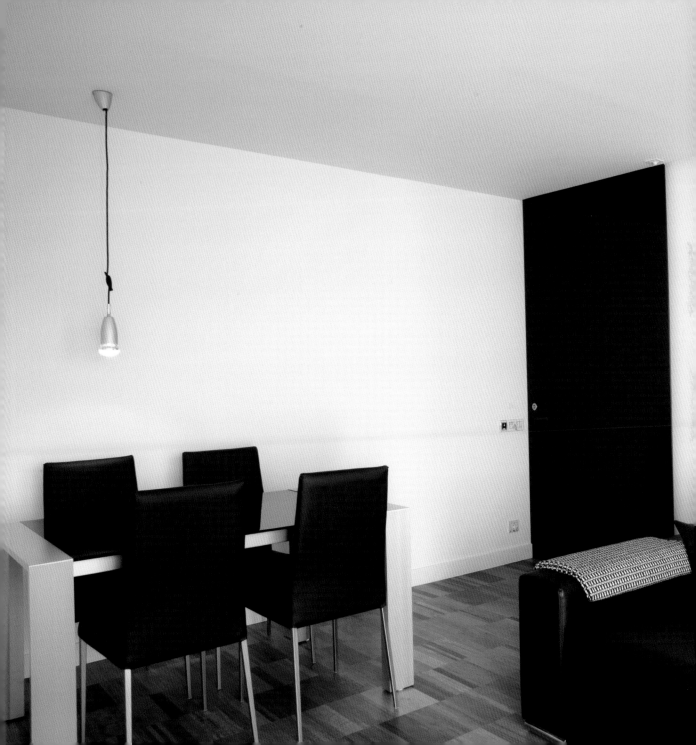

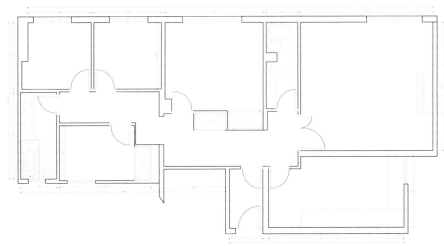

Floor plan before the renovation

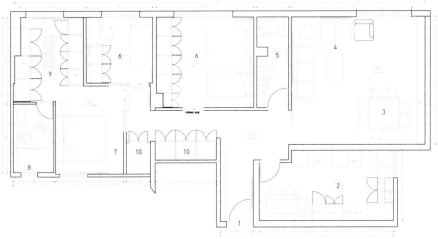

Floor plan after the renovation

1. Entrance
2. Kitchen
3. Dining room
4. Living room
5. Bathroom
6. Bedroom
7. Master bedroom
8. Master bathroom
9. Dressing room
10. Storage

The apartment is defined by the limited use of materials. The colors of the furnishings are neutral, pale and austere, and prominence is given to the ornaments chosen by the homeowner, such as this orange lamp.

The limited use of color results
in a simple, minimalist aesthetic.
The living-dining room of the
apartment includes a black glass
sliding door to match the sofa and
dining table.

68

WOVEN NEST

Architect: **Atmos Studio**
Location: **London, United Kingdom**
Photos: **Christoph Bolten/Recom Farmhouse, Atmos Studio**
Square footage: **759 ft² (70.6 m²)**

This apartment is defined by two elements that establish the design and personality of the interior: the openings in the top floor and the furniture integrated into a staircase. In the first case, a skylight and a small terrace with French doors manage to increase the natural light that enters the apartment and provide magnificent views of the city. The bedrooms, located on the top level, and the master bathroom are the main beneficiaries of the luminosity. The steps of the main staircase extend and become shelves, which complement the rest of the furniture positioned along the walls of the apartment.

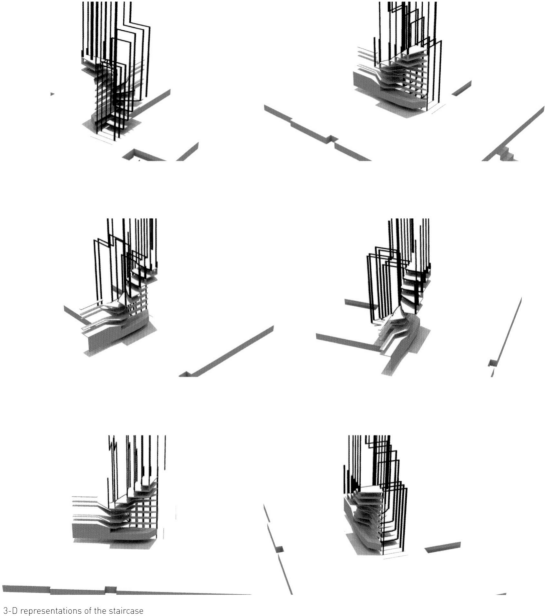

3-D representations of the staircase

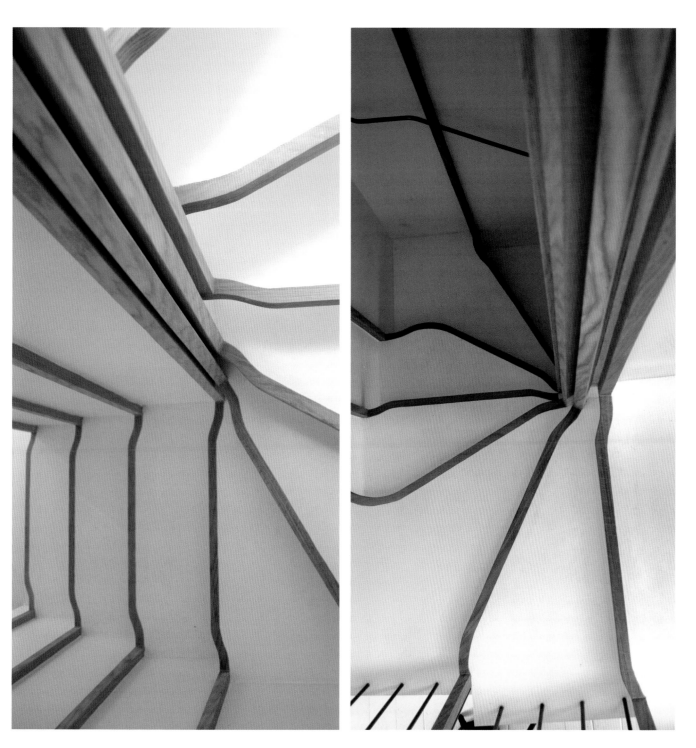

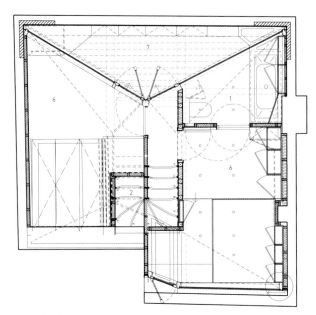

Upper level

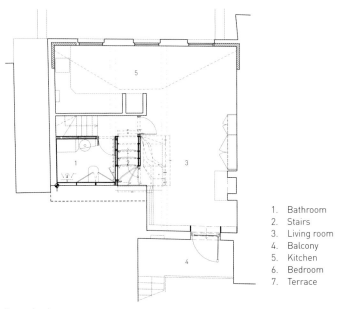

1. Bathroom
2. Stairs
3. Living room
4. Balcony
5. Kitchen
6. Bedroom
7. Terrace

Lower level

The use of glass in walls and roofs is a good option when a home is situated less than optimally, or is located among several buildings that prevent the entry of light. The glass walls must be appropriately thermally insulated.

69

RENOVATION IN BARCELONA

Architect: **Vora Arquitectura**
Location: **Barcelona, Spain**
Photos: **Adrià Goula**
Square footage: **1,033 ft² (96 m²)**

The owner of this apartment, a young bachelor, decided to highlight and reinforce the openness of the living spaces of the home with some minor modifications to the partition walls. The resulting space is more fluid, and the visual lines intersect the entire space thanks to the formation of semi-opened rooms. In this way, the movement of the sun is perceived throughout the day and natural light reaches more surface area. The central space is formed by the kitchen and the lounge, which are separated by a wall, flanked on one side by a large bookcase and on the other by the kitchen cabinet.

Floor plan before the renovation

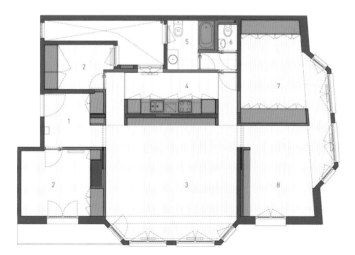

Floor plan after the renovation

1. Entrance
2. Bedroom
3. Living room/dining room
4. Kitchen
5. Bathroom
6. Washroom
7. Master bedroom
8. Study

Changes to the interiors of an apartment do not necessarily involve major construction work or large budgets. A simple change in the layout, as in this case, can offer a new perspective of the home.

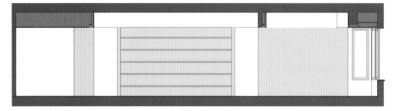

Section

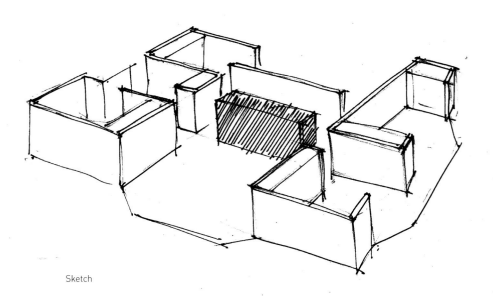

Sketch

70   Installing partitions that do not reach the ceiling or do not entirely enclose the space is a good option to lighten a space. It all depends on the degree of privacy you require.

EAST VILLAGE LOFT

Architect: **Fabrica 718**
Location: **New York, NY, USA**
Photos: **Sean Hemmerle**
Square footage: **645 ft² (60 m²)**

The renovation of this small loft in the popular East Village district has been a challenge for architects. Located in a former school building, they wanted to keep the height of the ceilings and some brick walls to preserve the original aesthetics of the building. It is precisely the height of the ceilings that has allowed the construction of a mezzanine that serves as a study or guest bedroom. The precise and judicious placement of the living room, kitchen and bedroom on the lower level result in functional, personalized spaces.

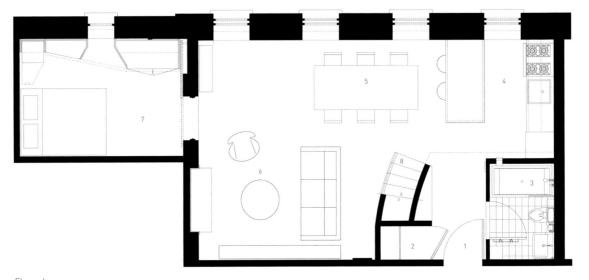

Floor plan

1. Entrance
2. Storage
3. Bathroom
4. Kitchen
5. Dining room
6. Living room
7. Bedroom
8. Staircase to the mezzanine

The renovation included custom furniture designed to maximize the storage space, such as the bedroom closets. On the walls, enough space has been left to display the owner's art collection.

71

A new staircase leads to the small mezzanine, situated over the entrance and the loft bathroom. By surrounding the upper level with a metal railing, an open and fluid ambience has been created that visually expands the apartment.

In spite of its small size, a judicious floorplan
allowed for the installation of a bathtub.
The simplicity of the tiles and built-in
storage creates a functional space.

PEARL STREET APARTMENT

Architect: **SPaN (Stonely Pelsinski Architects Neukomm)**
Location: **New York, NY, USA**
Photos: **Michael Moran**
Square footage: **600 ft² (56 m²)**

In this modest triplex located in New York, the square footage is maximized, and the use of the space is made more flexible with the installation of movable semi-transparent panels that change the configuration of the rooms throughout the day. For example, the first level goes from being a studio which is visually connected with the living and dining rooms, to being a spare bedroom with only one movement of a panel. The kitchen cabinets are also clad in these panels, giving the apartment a unified style. The extendable table and high bookshelf are examples of ways to optimize the use the available space.

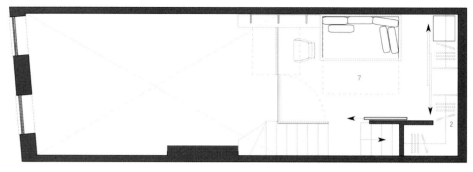

Level 1

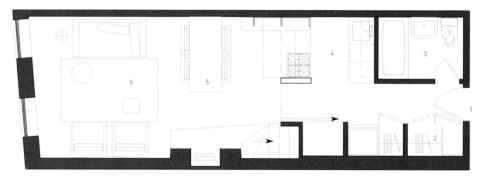

Level 0

1. Entrance
2. Storage
3. Bathroom
4. Kitchen
5. Dining room
6. Living room
7. Bedroom/study

The layout of duplexes or triplexes must be done so that vertical space is optimized, by positioning rooms such as bathrooms, kitchens and storage spaces under bedrooms and studies.

72

73 The versatility of furniture is a good way to take advantage of small spaces. Whether you opt for an extendable table, ottoman bed or sofa bed, the best use of the space is when it is dual purpose.

GRAPH

Architect: **Apollo Architects & Associates**
Location: **Tokyo, Japan**
Photos: **Masao Nishikawa**
Square footage: **925 ft² (86 m²)**

This apartment brings together living and working space. Reflecting the tastes of the owner, a cinematographer, the interior features a modern, urban style. A minimalist style that exemplifies these two concepts was established by opening up the space and adding original furniture. The result is a functional apartment, where each piece of furniture and each corner are used and play a role. The dark wooden floor and vertical blinds define the aesthetics of the home. White furniture has been installed in areas to create a contrasting color scheme.

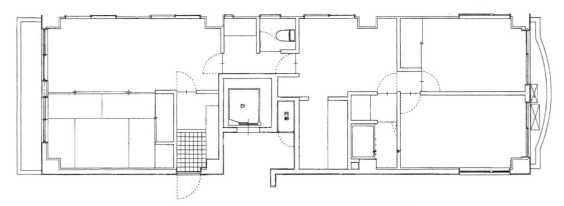

Floor plan before the renovation

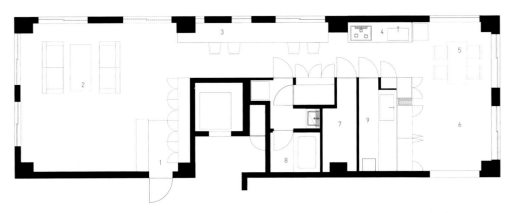

Floor plan after the renovation

1. Entrance
2. Living room
3. Study
4. Kitchen
5. Dining room
6. Bedroom
7. Darkroom
8. Bathroom
9. Powder room

74

The installation of wooden blinds reduces the entry of natural light into the space. In addition to managing the ambiance, they help to control energy consumption by regulating natural light and shade.

Placing some zones along a hall conserves space for use in other rooms. In this case, for example, the kitchen and some desks are aligned along one wall to allow the living room and the bedroom to be made larger.

75

GORANE

Architect: **Mis Mas**
Location: **Barcelona, Spain**
Photos: **Gaston Bertin**
Square footage: **699 ft² (65 m²)**

This 699 ft² (65 m²) apartment in Barcelona was renovated to maximize space and comfort for the family of five living there. To facilitate circulation, all the doors were converted into sliding doors. In the kitchen, part of the partition wall was replaced with a sliding window, improving the communication between the living room/dining room and the kitchen, and improving lighting. Other distinguishing elements can be found in the entrance; located between the childens' rooms, it was transformed into a playroom with the installation of custom furniture.

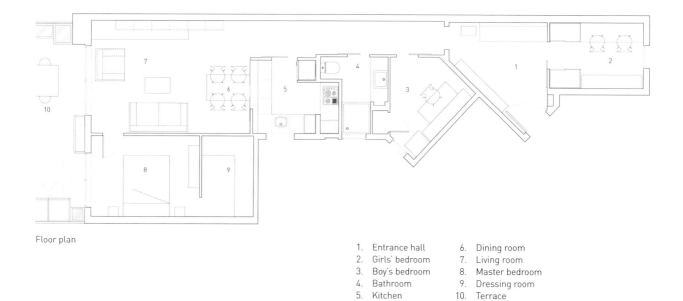

Floor plan

1. Entrance hall
2. Girls' bedroom
3. Boy's bedroom
4. Bathroom
5. Kitchen

6. Dining room
7. Living room
8. Master bedroom
9. Dressing room
10. Terrace

Removing doors in hallways and
fitting sliding doors improves the
flow between the different areas
of an apartment.

76

77 By opening the sliding door of the girls' bedroom, the hall becomes an annex of the room, which makes the room appear bigger.

Color has been introduced into this small apartment in cushions and through the new wallpaper, which combines different patterns.

BC+M

Architect: **Aurora Polo/Pensando en Blanco**
Location: **Hondarribia, Spain**
Photos: **Kini Aristegui**
Square footage: **757 ft² (70.4 m²)**

This apartment can be clearly divided into two zones: private and social. One goal was for each of the occupants to have a place to enjoy their free time, so small spaces were created within the home. This was achieved with a combination of oak and white lacquered MDF. The dressing room, the bedroom and the master bathroom are located in the private area. The last two are separated only by a sliding folding oak door. The social area contains three elements: the kitchen, the sofa and a bookcase, also framed by wooden panels.

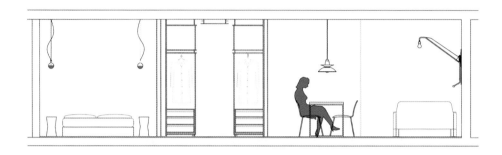

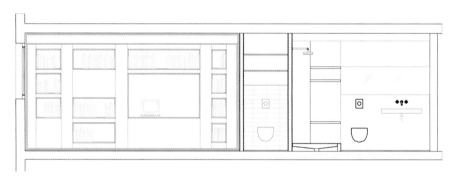

Sections

The bookcase serves as a link
between the kitchen and the sitting
area. It consists of four modules of
varying depths that perfectly match
the wooden panels and create
a central space for a desktop.

78

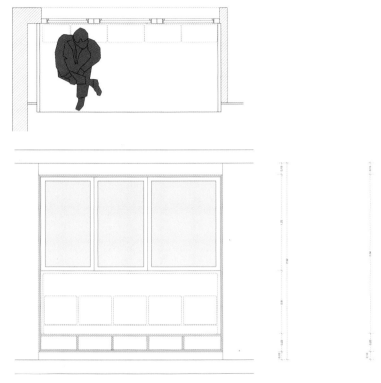

Construction details of the sofa

If it is not physically viable to join one room to the rest, a glass wall, either in whole or in part, will help to achieve visual connection to the rest of the apartment.

79

HOMAGE TO A DIRECTOR

Architect: **Ian Ayers, Francesc Zamora**
Location: **Barcelona, Spain**
Photos: **Francesc Zamora**
Square footage: **753 ft² (70 m²)**

This apartment located in the trendy, new Barcelona district dubbed "22@" underwent some changes to improve its distribution and adapt the decoration to the owner's personality. The budget was small, so the renovation was reduced to a minimum. The wall that enclosed the kitchen was torn down to integrate it with the living room. A high table now serves as a kitchen island and breakfast table. Bright colors on the walls modernize and personalize the interior. Paint was applied in vertical stripes in the bedroom, pistachio green was used in common areas, and all the colors were mixed in the entrance hall.

The finishes in the apartment were simple with an aseptic feel, and the kitchen was relegated to a narrow, dark corner. The change was achieved by tearing down a wall and painting the kitchen gray, resulting in a very modern look.

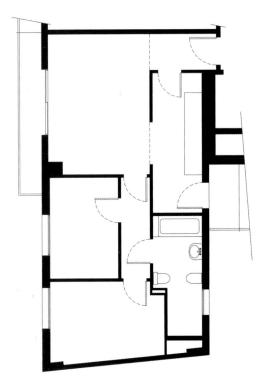

Floor plan before the renovation

Floor plan after the renovation

1. Entrance
2. Dining table
3. Living room
4. Kitchen
5. Utility room
6. Bedroom
7. Bathroom
8. Master bedroom
9. Balcony

One of the most effective ways improve lighting is to integrate spaces. In this case, the kitchen and the living room were combined, so the light from the balcony reaches the working area in the kitchen.

80

Sometimes you do not need a large investment or expensive construction work to radically change the look of an apartment. You only need ingenuity. Painting is one of the most effective solutions.

81

XS ORGANIZATION OF SPACES

Silvestrin Salmaso Architects © dieterphotodesigner.de

83

The absence of unnecessary divisions, especially partition walls or high walls, promotes mobility and visibility. Small homes and loft apartments are the biggest beneficiaries of this solution.

Pablo Uribe © Claudia Uribe

82

To enhance the feeling of space in a single area, install low cabinets in the kitchen and furnish the interior in a simple style. This way, you do not clutter the view and the interior appears to be larger and brighter.

AvroKO © Michael Weber

85

So that single spaces have a more youthful and dynamic style, you can choose to combine several solutions, such as building an attic or steps to separate levels and install each function on a different level.

Philippe Harden, Atelier 9 Portes © Philippe Harden

i29 | interior architects © i | 29 interior architects

84

Color can be a determining factor in the distribution of spaces. A central block of black in this Paris apartment serves to divide the main living area from the private areas.

86

Partitions can be walls, soffits, sliding doors, and even furniture. In this case, the furniture, in addition to containing a fireplace and a bookcase, serves as a screen separating the room from the entrance stairs.

Mandy Rafaty/Tag Front © Dean Pappas/Tag Front

UdA © Emilio Conti

88

When designing a home as a single space, it can be interesting and practical to include some panels or sliding doors for privacy in the bathroom or bedroom.

87

The choice of materials used to build the stairs and the architectural elements that create levels and enable the optimum use of the interior are determining factors that give the interior personality.

90

A traditional division of an ensuite bathroom can be transformed into an original space if the partitions are replaced by transparent glass partitions. The transparency transforms the space, unifies it, and enhances brightness.

89

So as not to occupy space that is required for other rooms, distribute the functions among the available area. An example might be to combine the kitchen and the dining room or place the study in the bedroom.

91

A double-height space is the perfect solution to install a new surface. Mezzanines maximize the use of space and the entrance of abundant light on the two levels.

s

LUDWIG ATTIC

Architect: **Craig Steely Architecture**
Location: **San Francisco, CA, USA**
Photos: **Tim Griffith**
Square footage: **1,097 ft² (102 m²)**

The original layout of the apartment was modified to enhance views of the Golden Gate Bridge and the rest of the city. In addition, changing the location of the bedrooms and opening up the spaces balanced the overall temperature of the apartment, as it was too hot on the south side and too cold on the north. This natural climate control meets the sustainability objectives of the architects, who prefer to use natural methods such as cross ventilation or the use of shade to achieve the thermal comfort of the interiors. This should help to reduce CO_2 emissions and achieve savings in energy consumption.

Floor plan

1. Entrance
2. Living room
3. Kitchen
4. Study
5. Dressing room
6. Bathroom
7. Powder room
8. Master bathroom
9. Master bedroom
10. Balcony
11. Dining room

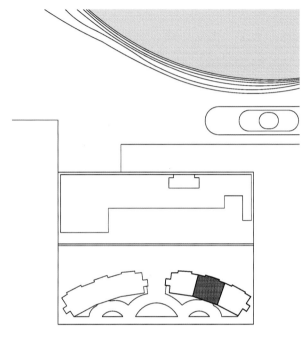

Site plan

92

It is appropriate to make the best use of the openings and views from the apartments. These openings to the exterior visually enlarge the rooms, for there is a relationship between the interior and the exterior of the apartments.

The environmental responsibility of architects is
evident in the use of wood from a fallen walnut
tree. This wood has been used for the blinds and
veneer of all the furniture in the apartment.

The bedroom and the master bathroom are merged into a single space. The absence of partitions makes for a larger room that allows for enjoying the views while taking a bath.

93

CARR APARTMENT

Architect: **Craig Steely Architecture**
Location: **San Francisco, CA, USA**
Photos: **Rien van Rijthoven**
Square footage: **1,400 ft² (130 m²)**

The decoration of this apartment features a luminous wall opposite a large window in the corner that offers stunning views of the city. The luminous wall, located on the east interior wall, is made of acid-etched glass. Behind it, LED lamps emit colored light according to the pixels in symphonic rock music videos from the 70s. The translucent glass blurs images and create visual effects that invade the living room. Thanks to this installation, the wall seems to move and modify the boundaries of the room.

94 Simple architectural plans emphasize other aspects of the interior design of an apartment, such as custom furniture, lighting or customized audio-visual effects.

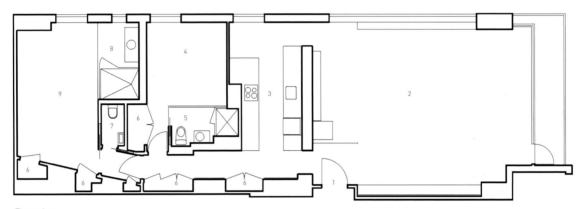

Floor plan

1. Entrance
2. Living room/dining room
3. Kitchen
4. Bedroom
5. Bathroom
6. Closet
7. Powder room
8. Master bathroom
9. Master bedroom

The doors, the wall panels and the furniture are custom-designed. Makassar ebony wood and Hawaiian koa provide comfort and balance an interior with a great presence of glass.

95

The use of straight lines and materials such as steel, gray panels, and translucent glass, give the kitchen a cold and almost industrial aesthetic.

LOFT IN HAMBURG

Architect: **GRAFT Gesellschaft von Architekten**
Location: **Hamburg, Germany**
Photos: **Ricardo Ridecos**
Square footage: **1,270 ft² (118 m²)**

The areas in this apartment are organized around an eye-catching walnut unit that departs from conventional partitions and regular divisions. Furthermore, the combination of neutral and pale colors and peripheral furniture and wood for the central construction creates dynamism. This module houses the kitchen and the bathroom, which unifies and centralizes the water zones and drainage facilities. A few recessed panels in the furniture allow you to close the bedroom and bathroom areas, providing privacy. The dining area and the living room are always connected.

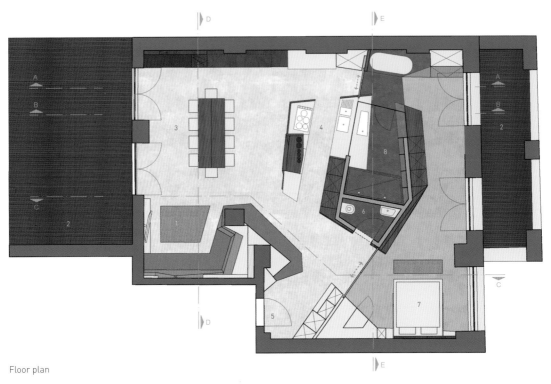

Floor plan

1. Living room
2. Terrace
3. Dining room
4. Kitchen
5. Entrance
6. Powder room
7. Bedroom
8. Bathroom

The construction of modules that bring together several functions are a solution in many apartments, as they rearrange the spaces, the circulation zones, and, since they are custom-made, they make much better use of space.

96

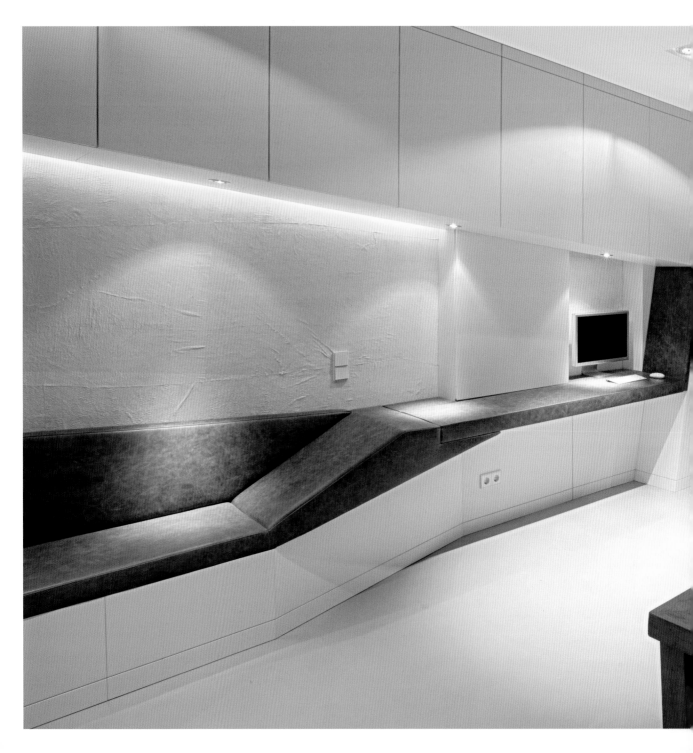

The module combines the kitchen, located around
a space that is a hallway, and the bathroom, with
another small washroom. The rest of the module
is used as a bookcase and storage space.

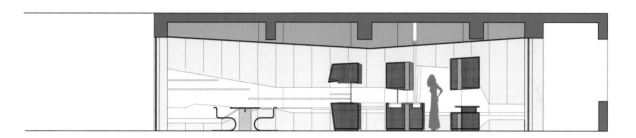

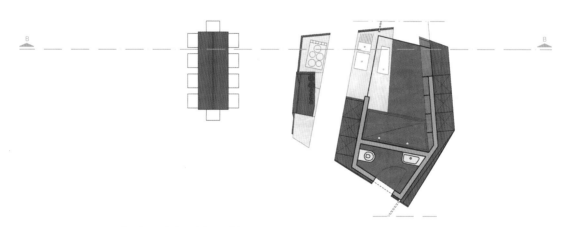

Section and plan of the module

97   The choice of materials can provide a different decoration to the interior of the home. The walnut of the central module, for example, is a warm and elegant wood that brings a unique touch to the apartment.

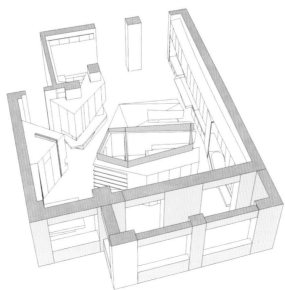

Axonometric of the open module

APARTMENT IN WULUMUQI STREET

Architect: **sciskewcollaborative**
Location: **Shanghai, China**
Photos: **sciskewcollaborative**
Square footage: **1,076 ft² (100 m²)**

The architects took advantage of an urban policy that allowed them to use red-tiles on the roofs of modern buildings to give a new character to this attic. The roof was elevated, allowing a glass skylight to be installed, improving the entry of light. The shape of the roof and the staircase leading to the mezzanine are distinctive elements of the decor. The pieces are superimposed and define a kind of spatial movement. These elements also have a functional component, as they conceal lamps and a ventilation system. In the rest of the apartment, a more conventional organization has been maintained.

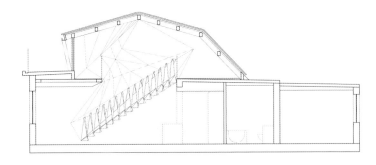

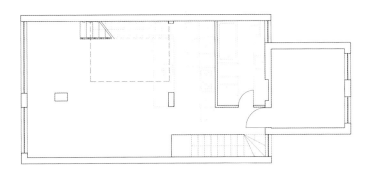

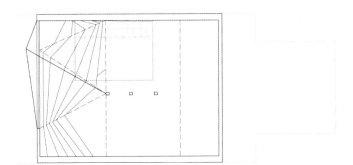

Section and floor plans

98

The first floor contains the living areas, the dining room and the kitchen. The unified space reduces privacy, but, with several functions sharing the same space, flow and the feeling of space are improved.

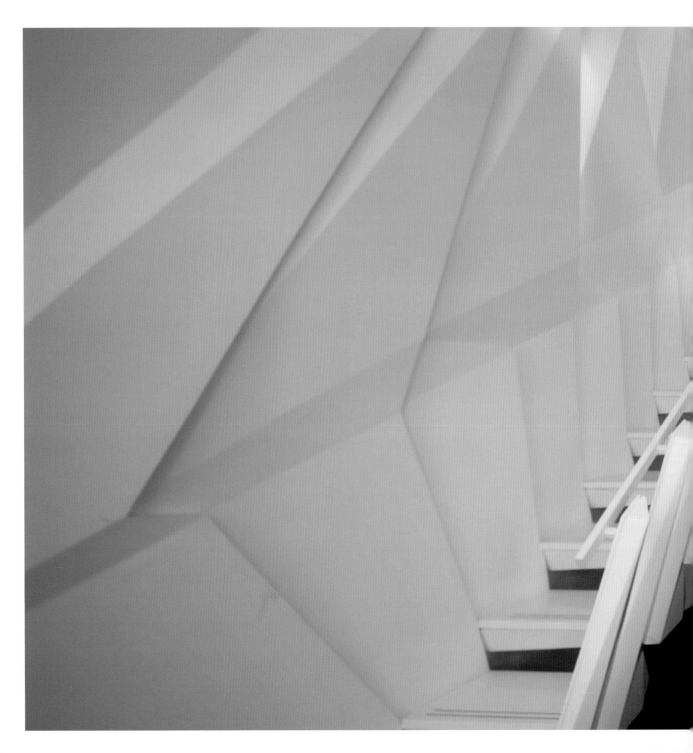

When the architectural elements take center stage, the character of a home changes. This staircase is the perfect example of how a functional piece has a sculptural dimension that defines the interior aesthetics.

This interior is defined by the color white, the wooden floor, and the stone from the kitchen and bathroom cabinets. This combination results in a simple and masculine aesthetic.

99

KANG DUPLEX

Architect: **Shichieh Lu/CJ Studio**
Location: **Taipei, Taiwan**
Photos: **Kuomin Lee**
Square footage: **1,400 ft² (130 m²)**

The plan of this duplex is inspired by the practice of origami. The apartment has a long, narrow floor plan that provided very poor natural lighting. To improve this, the wall of the rear facade was replaced with glass and the walls and ceilings were painted white. The floor is a continuous, bright and clear covering. The two levels are connected by transparent methacrylate stairs that multiply the light in the space. Besides contributing to the illumination of the apartment, two staircases create a loop that improves flow in the interior.

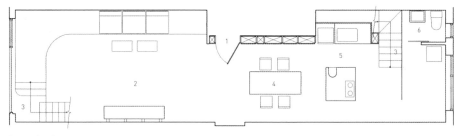

Lower level

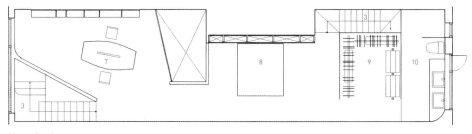

Upper level

1. Entrance
2. Living room
3. Staircase
4. Dining room
5. Kitchen
6. Powder room
7. Study
8. Bedroom
9. Dressing room
10. Bathroom

For visually larger spaces, you should use the same color range and the same type of decoration in all connecting spaces, even when they are on different levels.

100

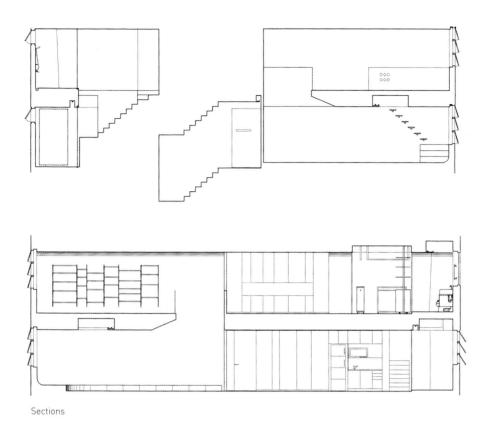

Sections

101 The installation of stairs in an apartment can be an opportunity to improve the flow between levels and achieve the integration of all the living spaces.

The kitchen maintains the decorative style of the apartment: straight lines, shiny finishes, and few details. Only a different color has been used to define the space.

HOME 07

Architect: **i29 | interior architects**
Location: **Amsterdam, The Netherlands**
Photos: **i29 | interior architects**
Square footage: **1,614 ft² (150 m²)**

This duplex was renovated to transform what was once a closed space with a double entrance hall and a hallway with many doors, into a spacious, open area, tailored to meet the needs of the family living there. In the kitchen, for example, the cabinets extend from floor to ceiling, and the decorative cut-outs in the white cabinet have beenprecisely cut with a laser. The color white is present in the ceiling and the floor, using an epoxy resin to increase brightness. The staircase, which is much lighter in weight now, lets natural light pass from the ceiling to the living room, located on the lower level.

The lack of walls between the dining room and the kitchen enhances the feeling of space and allows the family to be together while carrying out different activities. This layout is becoming increasingly common in homes today.

102

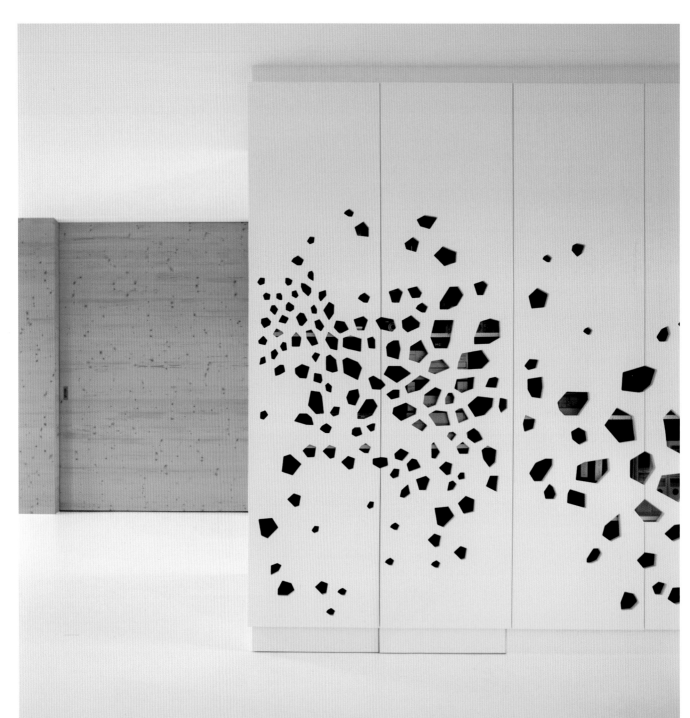

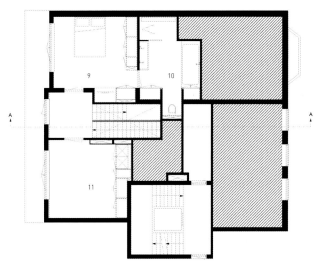

Upper level

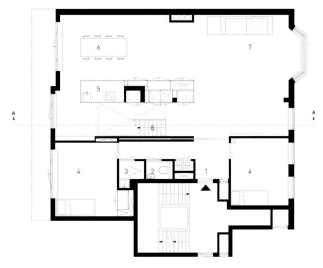

Lower level

1. Entrance
2. Powder room
3. Shower
4. Bedroom
5. Kitchen
6. Dining room
7. Living room
8. Staircase
9. Master bedroom
10. Master bathroom
11. Study

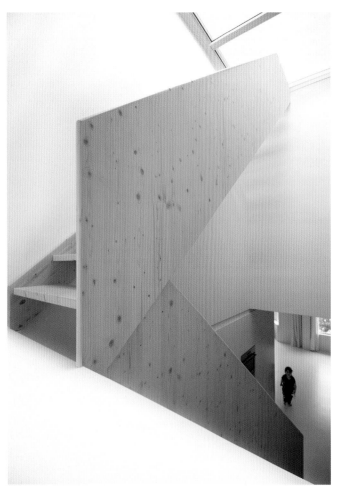

The installation of skylights is a solution for two-level apartments, as they allow the natural light to reach more recessed corners of the space. In this case, the renovated staircase serves as an atrium and increases the natural light in the interior.

103

The decoration of the apartment, based on the white floor and ceiling and on pine wainscoting in the closets, is repeated throughout the home, creating a stylistic unity that provides spatial coherence.

104

APARTMENT IN THESSALONIKI

Architect: **27 Architects**
Location: **Thessaloniki, Greece**
Photos: **27 Architects**
Square footage: **1,076 ft² (100 m²)**

The renovation of the apartment had to be done without changing any of the existing walls, and finally it was decided to change the furniture, which is a tool that transforms the formal and functional character of an interior. The living room and the dining area are big enough to allow for experimental design so, instead of selecting different pieces for each need, a single element that met all the needs was designed. It is a floor located 15.7 inches (40 cm) above the original which houses storage space, a bookcase, and other elements, such as lighting, a sound system and a video projector.

Floor plan

1. Entrance
2. Bookcase
3. Living room
4. Dining room
5. Bedroom
6. Study
7. Kitchen
8. Powder room
9. Bathroom

You can sit on, walk over or use the horizontal bookcase of the new furniture unit. The goal was to build a new floor to be used in different and unpredictable ways.

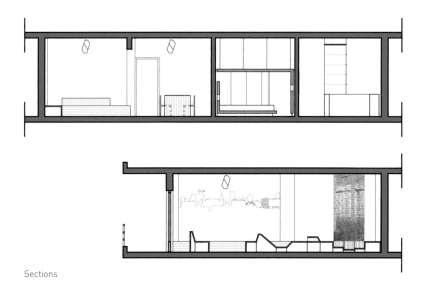

Sections

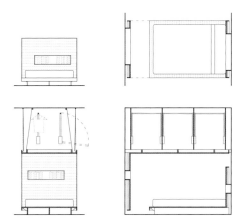

Construction details of the bedroom

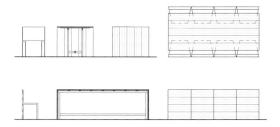

Construction details of the table

105 The design of artificial lighting is important in small spaces, as its location and quality can vary the perception of space. In this case, recessed lights in the furniture create a welcoming atmosphere.

LOFT IN MILAN

Architect: **LPzR Architetti Associati**
Location: **Milan, Italy**
Photos: **Chiara Pranzo-Zaccaria, Gabriele Pranzo-Zaccaria**
Square footage: **1,076 ft² (100 m²)**

This loft is located in a historic neighborhood near the church of San Cristobal. It was a very dark workshop, in bad shape because of dampness in the floor and walls. The objective, besides reorganizing the place and ensuring that the architectural elements were sound, was to allow in as much natural light as possible and to add a bathroom. The client asked for, in addition to luminosity, a contemporary, minimalist loft. The first priority was to delineate a courtyard, around which the main rooms are located, and promote the entry of light with skylights over the living room area. A relaxation area next to the courtyard, separated from the bathroom, was created.

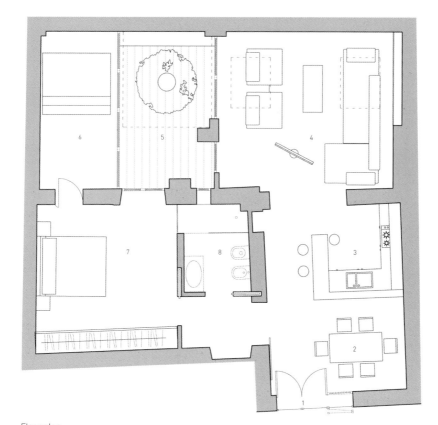

Floor plan

1. Entrance
2. Dining room
3. Kitchen
4. Living room
5. Courtyard
6. Relaxation area
7. Bedroom
8. Bathroom

The floor plan shows how the courtyard, in which a red maple has been planted, is the central element of the loft. The living room, the bedroom and the relaxation area are positioned around it. In addition to light, the courtyard contributes to the contemporary aesthetic that was sought.

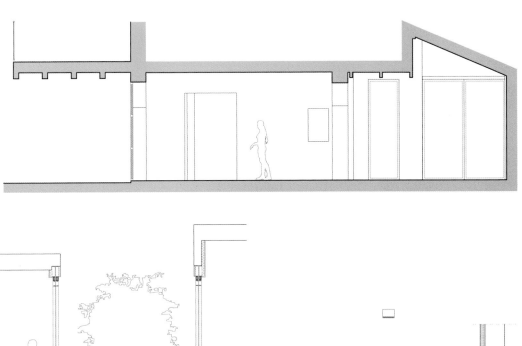

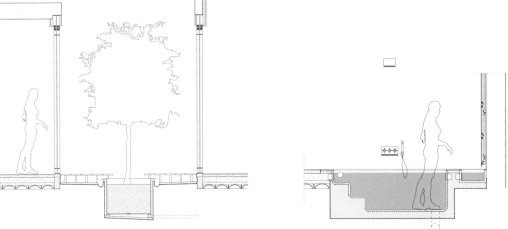

Sections

106

The wall that runs from the relaxation area through the courtyard and into the living room has been covered with pre-weathered titanium-copper-zinc panels. This provides continuity between the interior and the exterior spaces.

Because of the prevalence of the white in the apartment—including in the furniture—the floor, ceiling and walls are not delimited. Only a few small hits of orange break up the expanse of white.

Glass walls with sliding doors
between different rooms
improves the continuity of the
spaces. This solution is especially
suitable for homes with
courtyards and gardens.

107

WHITE APARTMENT

Architect: **Parasite Studio**
Location: **Timisoara, Romania**
Photos: **Andrei Margulescu, Parasite Studio**
Square footage: **1,614 ft² (150 m²)**

The jazz-loving owners of this apartment wanted to move away from the design of more conventional interiors without sacrificing any elegance, flexibility or functionality. The color white is the base upon which the furniture was placed, as a unified piece. The furniture and the partitions divide the areas and organize space, and instead of being static objects they define the apartment in a dynamic way. Some elements of the original apartment, such as the parquet flooring, have been kept because they add a touch of warmth to the interiors.

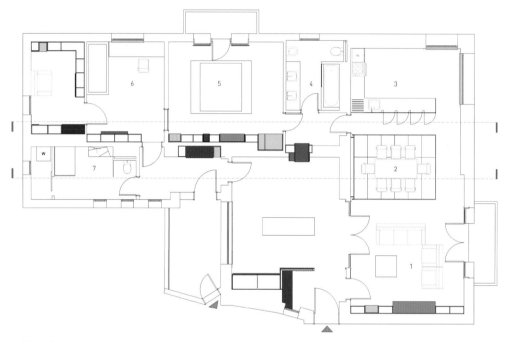

Floor plan

The floor plan shows the location of the custom
furniture. It is distributed in the entrance
hall, the lounge, the bedroom and the study.
Small touches of color break the uniformity
of the white and add a touch of freshness.

1. Living room
2. Dining room
3. Kitchen
4. Master bathroom
5. Master bedroom
6. Study
7. Bathroom

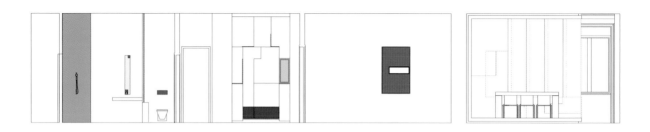

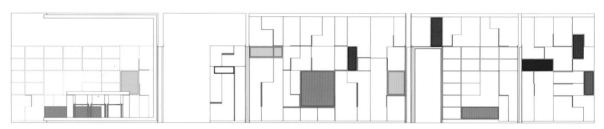

Sections

108

The kitchen is separated from the dining room by white movable panels. Aside from revealing the kitchen when opened, they increase the amount of natural light that reaches the space that the living room and the dining room share.

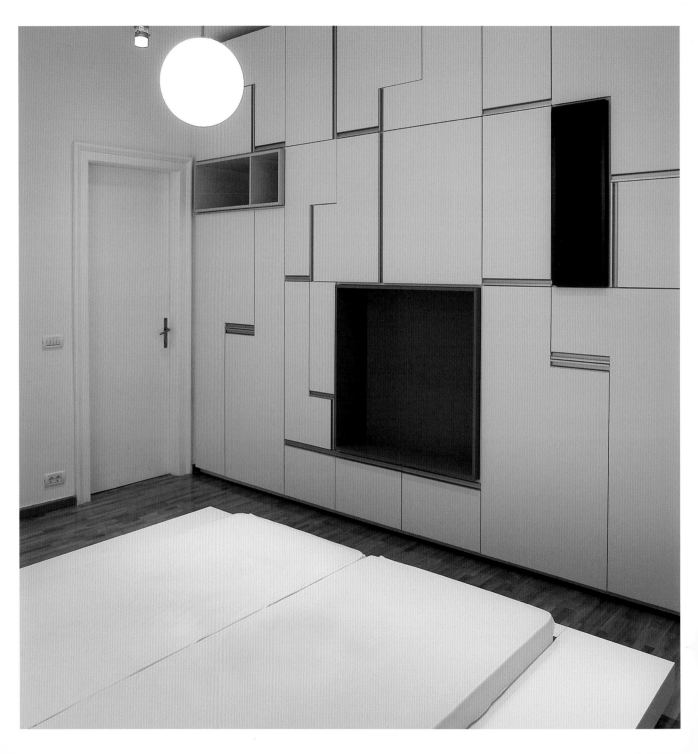

109

The bedroom is one of the areas in which the custom furniture is prominent, occupying the entire surface of the wall. The geometric shapes of the doors and the hints of color create dynamism and break the monotony of the white.

MB ATTIC

Architect: **Michele Gambato Architetto**
Location: **Padova, Italy**
Photos: **Michele Gambat, Cristian Guizza**
Square footage: **1,399 ft² (130 m²)**

The aim of this attic was to prioritize the views that can be seen from the windows. Also, the owners appreciate the importance of natural light, and wanted to maximize it. For this reason, it was decided to transform the layout and create a large open space in the lower level. The kitchen, the living room and the dining room occupy only one space separated by a partition, which has been maintained to ensure privacy in the bathroom and the entrance of the home. A lightweight spiral staircase leads to the upper level, where skylights continue to illuminate the interior.

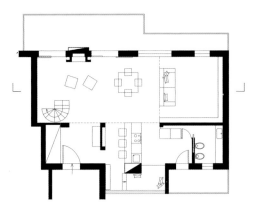

Lower level

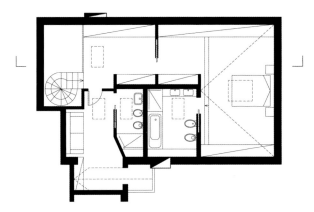

Upper level

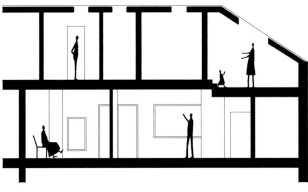

Section

110   The removal of walls allows daylight to penetrate into the spaces. If neutral tones and white colors are chosen for the walls and furniture, brightness is enhanced.

The slanted roof in many attics and top floor apartments gives the homes character. The right choice and layout of furniture will allow for sufficient space and a sense of roominess.

111

RETIREMENT IN SOUTH BEACH

Architect: **FORMA Design**
Location: **Miami Beach, FL, USA**
Photos: **Geoffrey Hodgson**
Square footage: **1,194 ft² (111 m²)**

The decoration of this apartment is based on the combination of the blue of the Atlantic Ocean and the purity of the white interiors. This color was chosen so as not to divert attention from the view of Biscayne Bay and the city skyline. If this mixture is added to the powerful light of Miami, the result is a bright and cheerful home. White is present in virtually every corner: ceramic floor, walls, furniture, etc. With the choice of different finishes and textures in the materials and furniture, you achieve an interior that is still sufficiently neutral, but with just enough personality.

At dusk, LED lights behind the wall panels change the aesthetics of the living room and transform it from an open space to a theatrical living room.

If you want to maximize the floor space of an apartment, avoid long corridors or halls. Part of this space can be used to enlarge other rooms.

112

Floor plan

1. Entrance
2. Kitchen
3. Dining room
4. Living room
5. Balcony
6. Bedroom
7. Master bedroom
8. Master bathroom
9. Bathroom
10. Closet

113

The layout of the apartment shows the importance the owners have given to each room. The bathrooms and the kitchen are smaller to dedicate extra space to common and rest areas.

114

To alleviate the monotony of white, make use of an accent color in a headboard or bedspread. This solution enables a quick and economic change.

APARTMENT
IN NEA SMIRNI

Architect: **Memos Filippidis, Marita Nikoloutsou/Mplusm architects**
Location: **Athens, Greece**
Photos: **Memos Filippidis**
Square footage: **1,291 ft² (120 m²)**

This apartment is located on the first and second floor of an apartment building. The privacy of the interior is ensured through a garden area and a perforated aluminum fence. There is a double-height living room, which gives the interior a solemn touch. To visually expand the space, one of the most common solutions in these cases has been applied: the spaces are unified and several functions are grouped together in the same area. The kitchen, the living room, the washroom and the garden are downstairs, which amplifies the feeling of space. The top floor is reserved for the bedroom and the bathroom.

The garden provides an outdoor space that gives
more versatility to the apartment. In summer the
living room is enlarged and life can be enjoyed
outdoors without sacrificing home comforts.

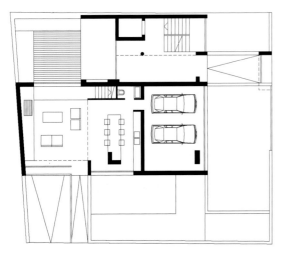

Lower level

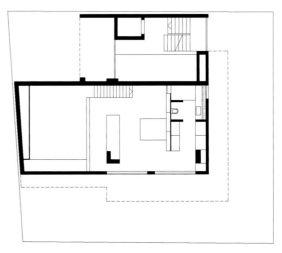

Upper level

The choice of materials and finishes is critical to the overall style of an apartment. Predominant colors like white, black and shades of gray provide an elegant and contemporary ambience.

115

116

The top floor has no closed walls
and the bedroom is directly
connected to the living room
without losing the privacy offered
by being located on a higher level.

DUMBO LOFT

Architect: **Jeff Etelamaki Design Studio**
Location: **New York, NY, USA**
Photos: **Jeff Etelemaki Design Studio**
Square footage: **1,097 ft² (102 m²)**

This loft, located in an old warehouse building, had a layout that did not make use of the space, and only had two exterior windows that allowed minimal entry of natural light. The main renovation was the demolition of the walls in the kitchen, thereby creating a large and rectangular space that conveys amplitude. In this unified space, different materials have been used in the walls and furniture to define and differentiate each function. For example, the kitchen is characterized by painted bricks, wallpaper, and glass tiles.

A useful resource for small apartments with high ceilings is to build elevated areas to make use of the space and separate the different functions without having to erect partitions.

117

Floor plan

1. Entrance
2. Dining room
3. Kitchen
4. Study
5. Living room
6. Bathroom
7. Bedroom

APARTMENT 8

Architect: **S.DREI Architektur**
Location: **Steiermark, Austria**
Photos: **Angelo Kaunat**
Square footage: **1,453 ft² (135 m²)**

The transformation of this apartment on the first floor of an old building converted an old, uninhabited environment into the future home of a family. The clients specified that there must be enough storage space and daytime rooms, but they also needed surfaces to display their art collection and extensive book collection. The solution was to use custom furniture, both integrated and exposed units, and to expand some rooms, such as the living room and dining room. The bedrooms have remained the same size so that more space could be dedicated to common zones.

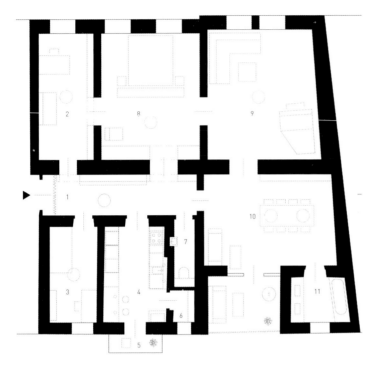

Floor plan

1. Entrance
2. Bedroom
3. Study/guest bedroom
4. Kitchen
5. Balcony
6. Utility room
7. Washroom
8. Master bedroom
9. Living room
10. Dining room
11. Bathroom

118

If you have wide hallways, take advantage and install narrow book shelves. Whether it is used to store books or shoes, functionality is gained without losing space.

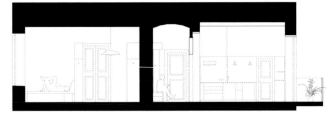

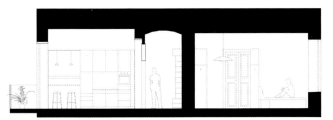

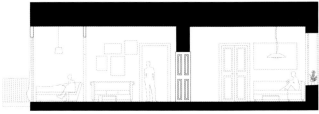

Sections

119   The lighting should take into account the functions of each room. The kitchen area must have bright light as it is a common work area. In the living room, however, lighting may be dim and soft.

U LOFT

Architect: **Garrick Jones/Ten to One Design Building**
Location: **New York, NY, USA**
Photo: **Garrick Jones**
Square footage: **1,194 ft² (111 m²)**

The Ten to One studio specializes in the renovation and construction of residential spaces. In this case, the restoration stands out for the U-shaped structure that is integrated into the center of the apartment, concentrating the common functions there. This leaves the remaining area free and the square footage is maximized. To improve the lighting and the perception of space, the height of the ceiling has been used to add windows to the upper part of the walls. The renovation has made the flow between the different rooms more fluid, especially in the daytime areas.

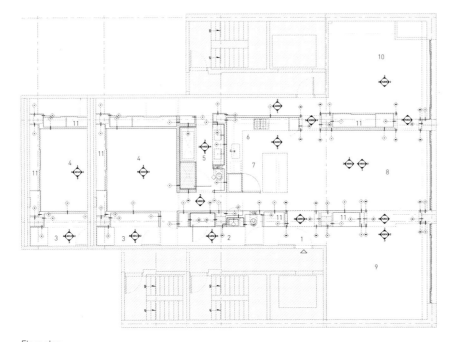

Floor plan

1. Entrance
2. Bathroom
3. Utility room/storage
4. Guest bedroom
5. Master bathroom
6. Kitchen
7. Dining room
8. Living room
9. Bookcase
10. Master bedroom
11. Closet

Well-connected rooms are essential in small spaces in order to achieve spatial continuity. Bringing the common areas together in a single area and separating the bedrooms is the usual solution to gain space and privacy.

120

Photomontages

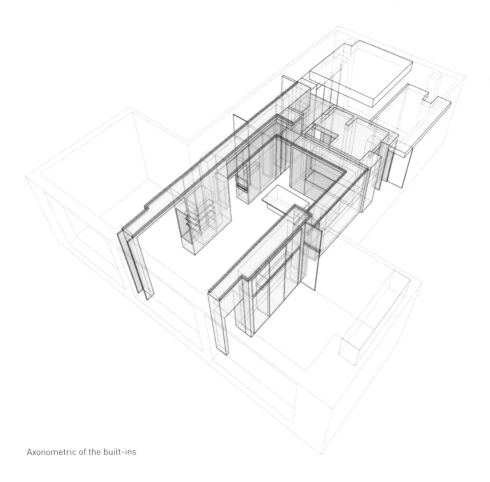

Axonometric of the built-ins

Positioning the built-ins around the edge of the rooms has a double function: to increase storage space and enhance the layout of the rooms. In this case, the U-shaped positioning stands out.

121

122 High ceilings can be used to construct mezzanines that increase the storage space or they can be maintained, to increase the feeling of spaciousness and light, as in this case.

REMODELING
IN CIUTAT VELLA

Architect: **YLAB Arquitectos**
Location: **Barcelona, Spain**
Photos: **Ciro Frank Schiappa**
Square footage: **1,399 ft² (130 m²) (+ terrace)**

The main objective of this renovation was to maintain the architectural elements typical of the building—arched passageways, wooden beams and vaulted arches—while transforming the interior into a modern space that could offer comfort and technology. The owner wanted a large space where they could greet and entertain friends, and for this reason the spaces were arranged so that the bedroom was at one end of the apartment and the kitchen-dining room at the other. The living room is between these two spaces and has an exit to a small terrace, which provides more natural light.

Changing materials and textures
can make an apartment unique.
In this case, for example, the
elegance of wood on the walls and
ceiling transforms the kitchen
and dining area.

123

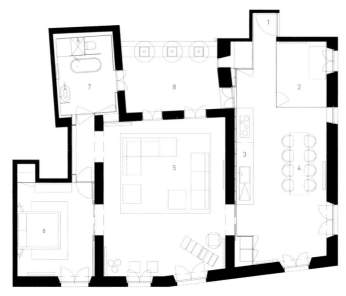

Floor plan

1. Entrance
2. Guest bedroom
3. Kitchen
4. Dining room
5. Living room
6. Master bedroom
7. Bathroom
8. Terrace

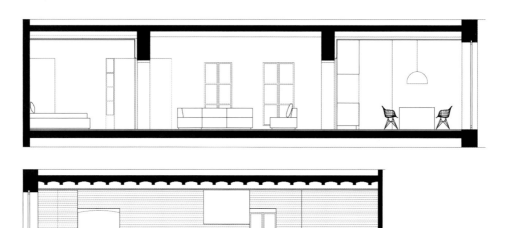

Sections

Colors play a major role in the definition of the spaces. If you want to achieve an airy space, such as in this room, multiply the brightness with a white ceiling, walls and furniture.

124

S
FINISHES

Boton © Boton

126

Fitted carpets in homes have fallen into disuse. However, advances in the composition of fibers have made materials easier to clean and more ecological, so they are no longer an option to be ruled out.

Naoki Terada/Teradadesign Architects © Yuki Omori

125

The use of synthetic materials is a good option to attain unique finishes that incorporate brilliance and new textures. They can be applied to both ceilings and walls without sacrificing the quality of regular paints.

One Plus Partnership © Ajax Law Ling Kit

127

Textile finishes are ideal for interiors. Depending on the type of fabric, cotton or wool, and colors, you can add warmth or cool down the rooms. Additionally, they can be more easily substituted than other materials.

129

Some architectural structures compulsorily determine the shape of the interior, such as this curved wooden ceiling of this houseboat. More original finishes are achieved by maintaining these structures.

Ronan Bouroullec
© P... and Ronan & Erwan Bouroullec

Hofman Dujardin Architecten © Matthijs van Roon

Wary Meyers Decorative Arts © John Meyers

Richardson

128

Use a different material to break the monotony that a single color creates. Wood is one of the best choices, as it adds warmth to the interior and integrates other pieces of furniture in the room.

130

Maintaining the original floor, if it is well preserved, is an option to consider when renovating a home. In many cases, you can keep the character of the architecture and achieve an interior with much more personality.

131

Although tile finishings with geometric patterns add vitality, they should not be used throughout the home to avoid visually saturating the space and so that the floor covering does not restrict the interior design.

132

It is advisable to install stronger materials in bathrooms and kitchens, the most frequented rooms. If you do not want to sacrifice originality, combine materials and arrange them according to the use that you will give to each space.

133

Mirrors can be used to visually increase the area of a bathroom. This is an original idea where a vital element in this room, usually a framed mirror, takes center stage and improves its usefulness.

134

In interiors with open spaces, the combination of materials is a good solution to define the use given to each surface. The contrast between the finishes is what identifies the separation of the rooms.

REMODELING

CASA BARBARA

Architect: **Barbara Appolloni**
Location: **Barcelona, Spain**
Photos: **Christian Schallert**
Square footage: **1,237 ft² (115 m²)**

This home, located in the Gothic Quarter of Barcelona, required a change in the existing distribution to convert the apartment into a spacious work and living area. To make the best use of the light that enters through the six balconies and the height of the ceilings, it was decided to get rid of the long corridor and break the original organization of spaces. The result was a large central room that gathers the public areas and serves as a boundary between the bedroom and study at one end, and the guest bedroom at the other. The conservation of original features, such as the doors of the balconies or the glass expanse of the dining room, creates a unique and cozy atmosphere.

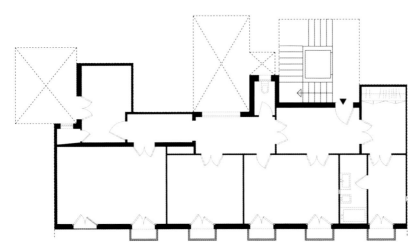

Plan before the renovation

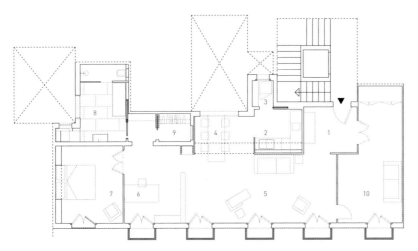

Plan after the renovation

1. Entrance
2. Kitchen
3. Pantry
4. Dining room
5. Living room
6. Study
7. Master bedroom
8. Bathroom
9. Dressing room
10. Bedroom

135

The apartment is organized around a large central room formed by the living room, the kitchen and the dining area. The ensemble is a continuous and flowing space, and also includes a working area.

Maintaining some features when
remodeling an apartment helps to
preserve the original atmosphere.
The doors of this home have been
retained, but stripped to reveal
the natural wood.

136

LE LOFT DES INNOCENTS

Architect: **Frédéric Flanquart**
Location: **Paris, France**
Photos: **Ludo Martin, Pascal Otlinghaus**
Square footage: **861 ft² (80 m²)**

A fire in the building defined the rehabilitation of this loft with 360° views over the city of Paris. The staircase acted as a chimney, and the fire burned almost the entire top floor. After the incident, the only thing worth preserving were the wooden beams. After 18 months of work, a completely renovated and updated home was inaugurated. The recovered beams mark the lines of the space and are reminiscent of the past, and the colors (red, gray and white) create a contemporary and modern ambience. Overall, the complexity of the rehabilitation of the apartment shows simplicity and lightness.

137

The sloping roofs of this apartment can make the space seem visually smaller. To counteract this, all the windows and skylights have been optimally positioned and all the walls have been painted white.

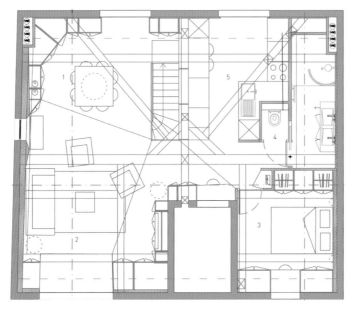

Floor plan

1. Dining room
2. Living room
3. Bedroom
4. Bathroom
5. Kitchen

138

Custom cabinets are one of the solutions that make the most efficient use of the area available in an apartment. They are particularly suited to small spaces, and they also integrate seamlessly into the decor.

The wooden beams have a dual role: they function as important structural elements and also give a personal aesthetic to the ensemble, which tempers the coolness of modern design with warmth of the wood.

139

MORGAN RESIDENCE

Architect: **Tang Kawasaki Studio**
Location: **New York, NY, USA**
Photos: **Björg Magnea**
Square footage: **1,506 ft² (140 m²)**

This project was carried out in an industrial building in Greenwich Village. The original space had windows on the north and south facades and stood out for its vaulted red brick ceilings. The ceilings were left exposed to maintain the industrial aesthetic. The floor is stripped white oak that has been coated with a protective layer. The radiators and storage units under the windows have been closed with white perforated lacquered carpentry, keeping them well hidden. To enhance luminosity and integrate the functions in the large central space, the walls have also been painted white.

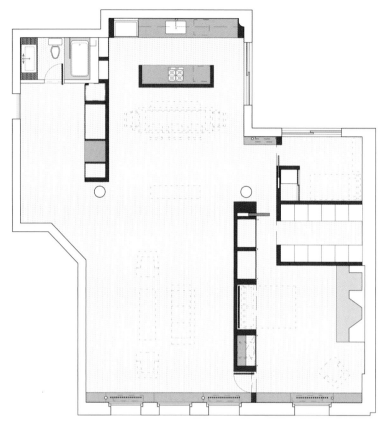

Floor plan

One way to avoid obstructing the view in open spaces is to build shelves. These elements are fused with the walls and are integrated into the distribution of spaces as if they were walls or partitions.

140

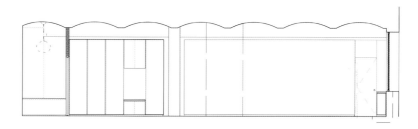

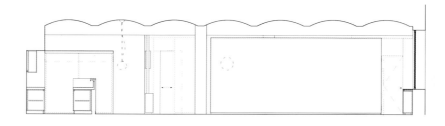

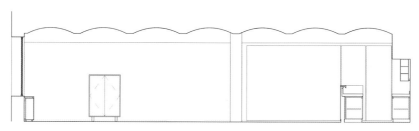

Sections

One of the best solutions to hide a kitchen in a loft, especially in minimalist spaces, is to build a small wall that will conceal it from other spaces.

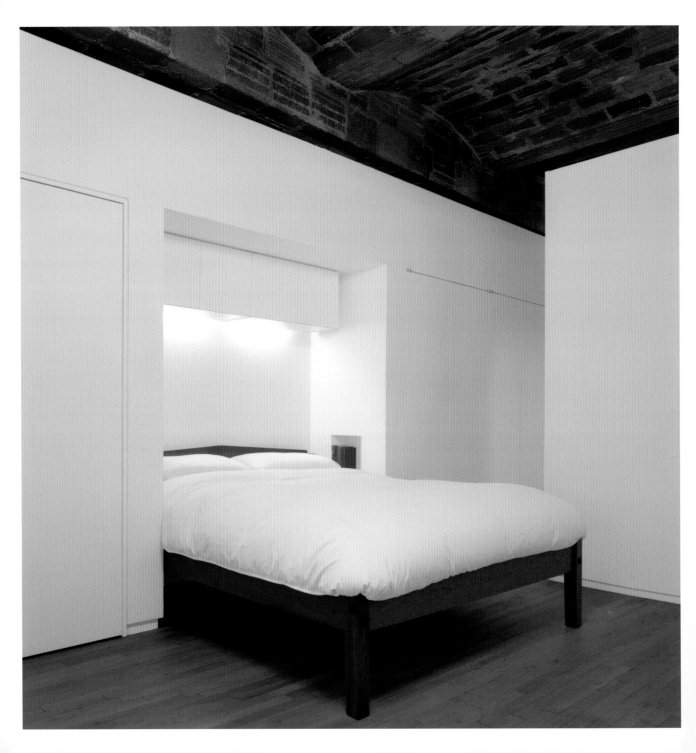

ATTIC B&L

Architect: **Michele Gambato Architetto**
Location: **Padova, Italy**
Photos: **Michele Gambato**
Square footage: **1,560 ft² (145 m²)**

The renovation of this apartment had to keep the shell intact while achieving a suitable division of the rooms for the needs of the owners. The owners wanted to maintain the unique sense of space, so the architects decided that the light brick walls and beams of the roof were to be left exposed and glass would be used for the majority of partitions. A magnificent metal staircase with an integrated bookcase was built to connect the two levels. The result is a yet-to-be-furnished apartment featuring an elegant contrast between the new partitions and old walls.

Upper level

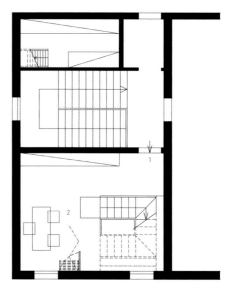

Lower level

1   Entrance
2   Study
3   Living room
4   Dining room
5   Kitchen
6   Master bedroom
7   Bedroom
8   Shower
9   Master bathroom
10 Washroom
11 Terrace

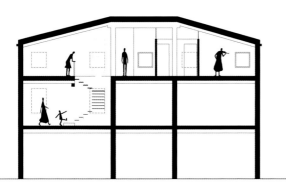

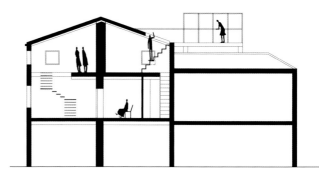

Sections

141

The fusion of architectural elements, in this case a staircase with an integrated bookcase, can create exciting new possibilities. They can become sculptural elements that define the interior aesthetics.

142 In renovations, some elements become central pieces, whether this was the intention or not. In this case, the metal staircase, the brick walls and the wooden beams complement each other to create a unique and powerful visual space.

MARCO POLO APARTMENT

Architect: **Carola Vannini Architecture**
Location: **Rome, Italy**
Photos: **Filippo Vinardi**
Square footage: **1,291 ft² (120 m²)**

The main objectives of the architects were to modify the layout of the apartment and to radically change the decor. To accommodate the new needs of the owner, the living room spaces were opened up to convey the feeling of continuous space. To reinforce this idea, the kitchen was located partially behind a brick wall painted green that does not reach the ceiling. The only private spaces are the ones corresponding to the rest areas: the bedroom, the office, the bathrooms and the guest room. The decor stands out for vibrant and elegant colors that form a contemporary interior.

143   The renovation of an apartment is the perfect opportunity to include custom elements. In this case, the gap between the living room and the kitchen has been used to insert a long plank that serves as a shelf and as a table.

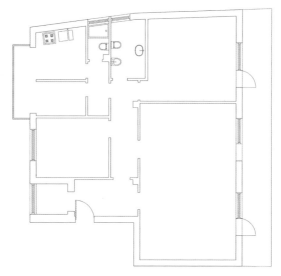

Floor plan before the renovation

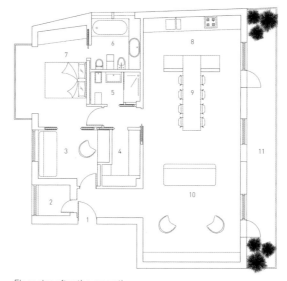

Floor plan after the renovation

1. Entrance
2. Closet
3. Guest bedroom
4. Dressing room
5. Bathroom
6. Master bathroom
7. Master bedroom
8. Kitchen
9. Dining room
10. Living room
11. Balcony

APARTMENT IN MADRID

Architect: **Nacho Polo Interior Designer**
Location: **Madrid, Spain**
Photos: **Antonio Terrón, Andrea Savini**
Square footage: **1,184 ft² (110 m²)**

This apartment has been renovated by the owner, the designer Nacho Polo. The major change has been the recovery of the original essence of the apartment, dating back to the 19th century. This has been done by recovering the floors and the woodwork, as well as the iron radiators and the ceiling plasterwork. It also does away with some of the small and dark rooms to give priority to larger spaces. Since the apartment has only one exterior facade, it was decided to locate the living room in the closest rooms and leave the bedrooms, the bathrooms and the dressing room in the interior zone.

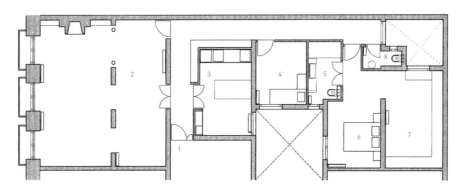

Floor plan after the renovation

1. Entrance
2. Living room
3. Kitchen
4. Guest bedroom
5. Bathroom
6. Master bedroom
7. Dressing room
8. Powder room

144

If there is not much natural light in a space, you can use white, which is the color that best reflects light, to increase the brightness. Installing mirrors multiplies its effect.

145 The furniture and decorative objects chosen must show the owner's personality and tastes. Otherwise, you run the risk of displaying a collection of antiques and prestigious furniture that lacks a theme.

Using a combination of white and black is a good resource for decorating an interior. It can be applied in alternating vertical stripes, or be used in two-color prints in some corners or specific objects.

146

APARTMENT IN CHUECA

Construction: **DEDENTRO**
Decoration: **Cristina Ros**
Location: **Madrid, Spain**
Photos: **Germán Sainz, DEDENTRO**
Square footage: **968 ft² (90 m²)**

The apartment, owned by Spain Select (www.spain-select.com), a company that rents out luxury apartments, has undergone a complete renovation that has improved the layout of the interior. The construction work has transformed an apartment of rooms located along a narrow corridor, into a bright and spacious home. The kitchen, which used to be at one end of the apartment and separated from the other rooms, is now part of the large dining room. The renovation has left two bedrooms, which are now larger and make better use of the space, with custom closets. A new bathroom has also been added to the apartment.

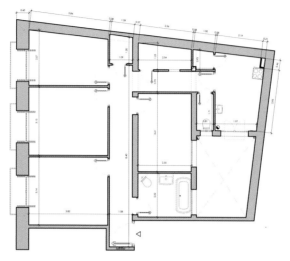

Floor plan before the renovation

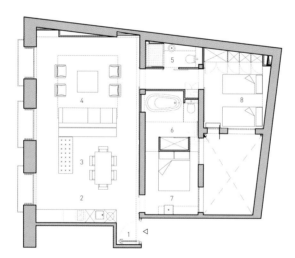

Floor plan after the renovation

1. Entrance
2. Kitchen
3. Dining room
4. Living room
5. Bathroom
6. Master bathroom
7. Master bedroom
8. Bedroom

147 In integrated or specific areas, the decor of the kitchen can adapt and merge with the greater area. In this way, the space is unified and a sense of spaciousness is created.

Interior elevations

148

The combination of furniture in different styles and from different periods creates a dynamic space with personality, especially in a renovated apartment where you can see the passing of time and traces of the original architecture.

The bathrooms in this apartment combine
elements of different styles. Some are modern,
such as the fixtures and fittings, some are
rustic, such as the sink, and some are classic,
such as the bath in the ensuite bathroom.

RENOVATION OF AN APARTMENT IN PAMPLONA

Architect: Íñigo Beguiristáin
Location: Pamplona, Spain
Photos: Iñaki Bergera (www.bergeraphoto.com)
Square footage: 1,291 ft² (120 m²)

The renovation of the apartment attempted to go beyond the conventions of the typical layouts in family apartments. The architects wanted to show how ingenuity and craftsmanship can enhance the perception of space and increase the feeling of spaciousness. In one of the day-use areas, all partitions were removed, creating long, attractive diagonal visual lines and improving the flow between these spaces. The bedrooms—the occupants' private areas—are larger and not connected to each other, which promotes rest and calm.

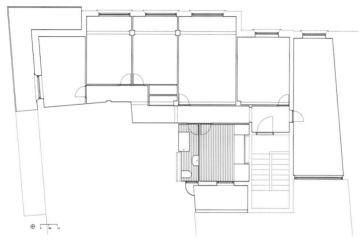

Floor plan before the renovation

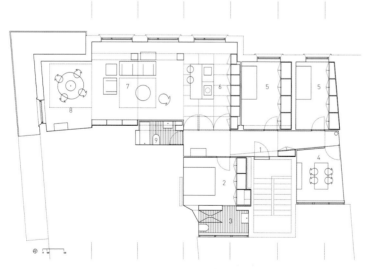

1. Entrance
2. Master bedroom
3. Master bathroom
4. Study
5. Children's bedroom
6. Kitchen
7. Living room
8. Dining room
9. Bathroom

Floor plan after the renovation

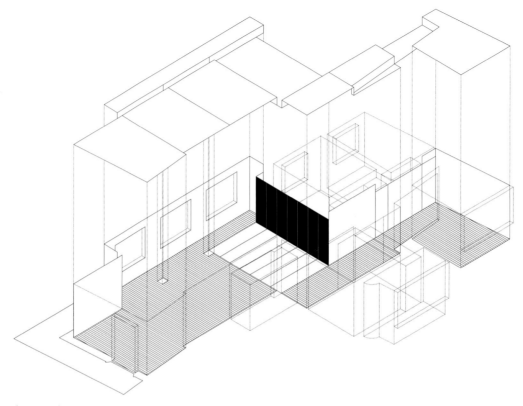

Axonometric

The layout of an apartment, when possible, should be planned according to the needs of each family. In this case the day-use areas have been located in one space, separated from the bedrooms.

149

The white walls and wooden floor define the overall aesthetic, which is broken up by pieces of furniture in bright colors that add vitality and originality to the decor of the home.

150

Natural lighting is perfect in small rooms, such as bathrooms. In this case, a translucent white curtain ensures that light enters without sacrificing the necessary privacy.

CONNOR RESIDENCE

Architect: **Emilio Fuscaldo, Imogen Pullar/Nest Architects**
Location: **Elwood, Australia**
Photos: **Jesse Marlow**
Square footage: **1,291 ft² (120 m²)**

The interiors of this home were designed to create a welcoming atmosphere. The client, a film producer, was involved in the process of defining the volumes and forms of spaces that the new floor plan should have. The idea of inserting new elements into the space was used, thus reinforcing the original art deco design of the home. The elements that were added were pieces of furniture understood as active elements of the home. The furniture that connects the bedroom to the living room, for example, defines the look of these two spaces. In the rest of the home, shelves in the same wood were installed.

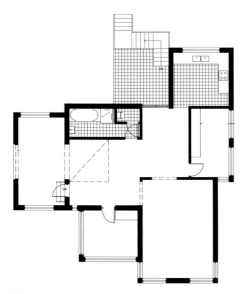

Floor plan before the renovation

Floor plan after the renovation

1. Entrance
2. Bathroom
3. Bedroom
4. Dining room
5. Study
6. Living room
7. Kitchen
8. Terrace

151

Always take into account the visual trajectory and flow through rooms to create a more comfortable and attractive interior. In this case, the opening from the entrance into the living room visually extends both rooms.

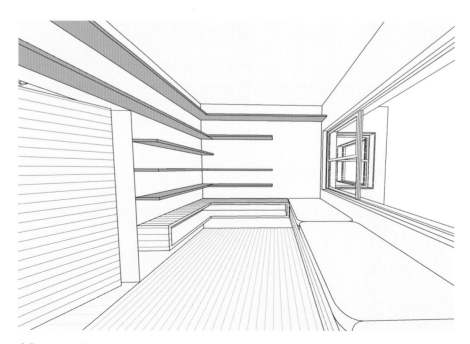

3-D representations

A variety of warm wooden elements are
distributed throughout the apartment to cheer
up the interior. Each piece is simple, but with an
imposing presence, and they arouse curiosity.

152

Furniture can be constructed from recycled wood. In this case, two varieties of eucalyptus wood were chosen. The planks were classified according to their measurements in order to facilitate the construction of each cabinet or shelf.

LOFT IN THE EIXAMPLE DISTRICT

Architect: **Data AE**
Location: **Barcelona, Spain**
Photos: **René Pedersen**
Square footage: **1,560 ft² (145 m²)**

Integrating different uses into a compact volume was the basis for the renovation of this bright penthouse, originally segmented into small rooms. On the first floor, walls were removed, and a long structure was installed that makes use of the space by bringing various functions together, such as the kitchen and a large bookcase. The bedroom, the study and the dressing room are located on the top floor, and they are opened or closed by sliding panels. By freeing the space, better use is made of light and the space has direct contact with the terrace.

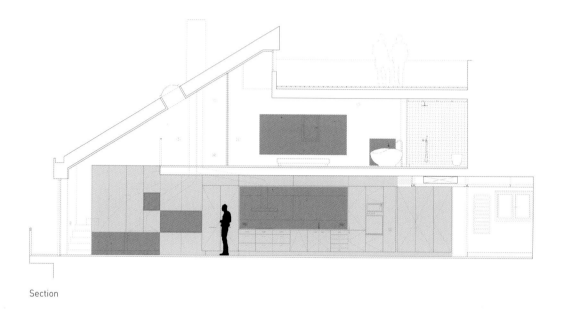

Section

Using a single architectural element—such as a piece of furniture built along the expanse of one wall—to unite areas of different functions is a great way to free up space, since, in this way, you won't have to build a separate unit for each area.

153

Although the concept of a loft implies that the functions should be gathered in a single unpartitioned space, you should allow for some privacy, whether it is in the bathroom or the guest rooms.

154

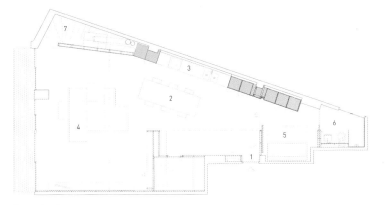

Lower level

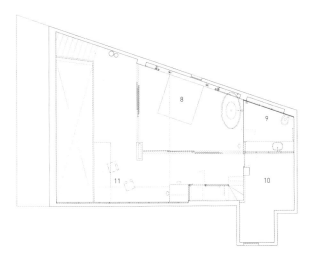

Upper level

1. Entrance
2. Dining room
3. Kitchen
4. Living room
5. Guest bedroom
6. Bathroom
7. Staircase
8. Master bedroom
9. Master bathroom
10. Dressing room
11. Study

Mobile partitions must be constructed with lightweight materials so that they can be moved easily and integrated seamlessly into the spaces. Permanent partitions can be made from translucent materials such as glass or screens.

155

APARTMENT IN ILION

Architect: **LKMK Architects**
Location: **Athens, Greece**
Photos: **Louisa Nikolaidou**
Square footage: **1,237 ft² (115 m²)**

The objective of this project was to combine two small apartments to create a new home for a family with children. Extension projects need not impose a limitation, and, in this case, room was left for experimentation. The simplicity of the floor plan has resulted in a harmonic, light space, with a logical distribution: a day-use area that includes the kitchen, dining and living rooms, and the bedrooms, separated by a small hall.

The combination of the kitchen, the dining room and the living room into one area does not only save space, but it creates a pleasant sense of continuity.

156

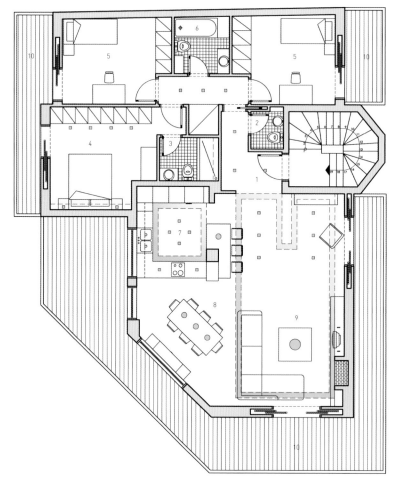

Floor plan

1. Entrance
2. Powder room
3. Master bathroom
4. Master bedroom
5. Bedroom
6. Bathroom
7. Kitchen
8. Dining room
9. Living room
10. Terrace

157

When integrating several rooms into one space, the same materials and same type of furniture can be chosen. This will accentuate the stylistic uniformity and generate spatial coherence.

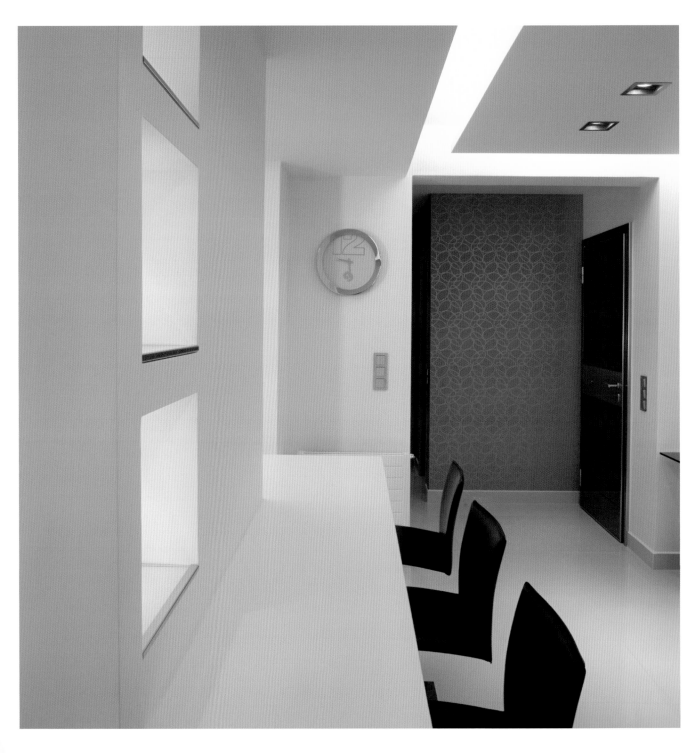

The master bedroom has a large built-in closet fitted with a strip of smoked glass in the sliding doors. This breaks the monotony of the monochromatic doors and visually expand the room.

If you have more than one bathroom, you can give each of them their own personality. In this case, colors and designs are different.

158

X LOFT

Architect: **Carola Vannini Architecture**
Location: **Rome, Italy**
Photos: **Filippo Vinardi**
Square footage: **1,291 ft² (120 m²)**

The renovation of this apartment is summarized in one action: the removal of a corridor that darkened the rooms. Initially, the rooms were organized along this corridor, and the renovation transformed it into a long, bright space that creates large and interesting perspectives through a structure of beams and columns. Instead of camouflaging the structure, it was painted bright red and integrated into the space so that it serves as a dividing element for each zone. The furniture design, especially in the kitchen, helps to give this open space a contemporary aesthetic.

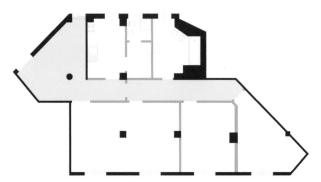

Floor plan before the renovation

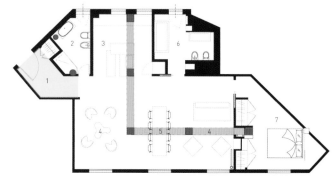

Floor plan after the renovation

1. Entrance hall
2. Bathroom
3. Kitchen
4. Living room
5. Dining room
6. Master bathroom
7. Bedroom

The plans show how eliminating the corridor created an open space. In addition, this new layout has reduced the size of the entrance hall, which was originally too big, and has added a new bathroom.

A new partition wall has been erected in the
new bedroom that leaves a gap behind the
bed. This wall includes new lighting that
creates a more comfortable and cozy space.

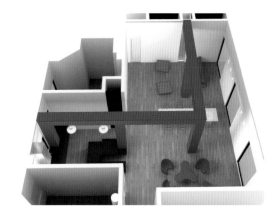

Perspectives

Societal changes cause changes
in floor plan trends. Entrance
halls, for example, used to be
made quite large, but now in
an effort to make better use of
square footage, they tend to be
smaller. In this case, a bathroom
has been added. Extending the
living room or building a dressing
room are other options too.

159

J LOFT

Architect: **Plystudio**
Location: **Singapore, Singapore**
Photos: **Stzernstudio**
Square footage: **1,291 ft² (120 m²)**

The remodeling of this attic was highly transformative. In this typical post-war space, a contemporary interior has now been achieved. After the demolition of existing partitions, which helped optimize the lighting, a series of plywood boxes were installed to make up the different areas of the home. These pieces—furniture and partitions—work together to create open spaces that function independently. Only private areas have doors. This furniture takes up only 6.5 ft (2 m) of the 20 ft (6 m) wide space, so it does not reduce the width. A mezzanine was built in order to take advantage of the height of the space.

1. Entrance
2. Kitchen
3. Bathroom
4. Bedroom
5. Dining room
6. Study
7. Living room
8. Mezzanine

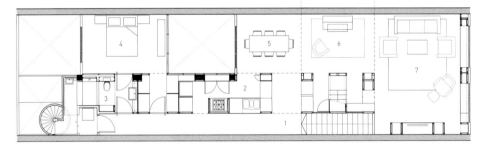

Floor plans

Diagrams of furniture

160

One option to lower the price of custom furniture is to use plywood instead of solid wood. This type of material offers good quality, sacrificing neither beauty or durability.

When you create a mezzanine, you should consider the effect on the lighting and the airiness of the resulting spaces. The solution is to build partitions that do not reach the ceiling and allow flow between levels.

161

YALETOWN LOFT

Designer: **Kelly Reynolds Interiors**
Location: **Vancouver, Canada**
Photos: **Chad Falkenberg**
Square footage: **999 ft² (92.9 m²)**

The aesthetic of this apartment blends the typical details of an industrial loft with other elements that give it an individual feel. The home has gone from having two bedrooms and two bathrooms to being a large suite with a large kitchen with everything a chef could ever want. The kitchen, combined with the dining area, opens up to a large hall where the owner receives his friends. Brick and concrete on the walls, also present in the floor albeit with a more polished finish, emulate the "cold" look of an industrial loft, while the wooden beams in the ceiling bring a touch of comfort and warmth.

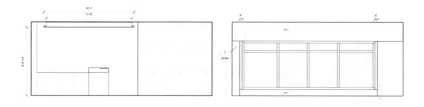

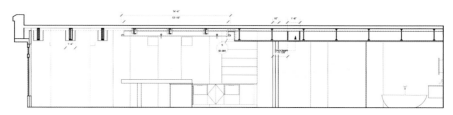

Sections

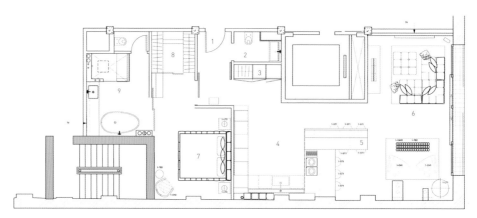

Floor plan

1. Entrance
2. Washroom
3. Storage
4. Kitchen
5. Dining room
6. Living room
7. Bedroom
8. Dressing room
9. Bathroom

162 When designing an industrial-style look, avoid excessive decorative objects that could clutter the rooms. Wall and floor materials should be distinctive enough to define the environment.

White and gray are the predominant colors in the bathroom of the bedroom. To break the monotony and add a hint of sophistication, violet was used in the shower and a wooden bathroom cabinet was installed.

163

APARTMENT IN GRACIA

Architect: **Bárbara Aurell**
Location: **Barcelona, Spain**
Photos: **Ana Madrid**
Square footage: **753 ft² + 215 ft² (70 m² + 20 m²)** (terrace)

This apartment, located in the base of a of building, shows that every space has potential and that a good idea is more important than a big budget. It was impossible to make use of any element of the original structure, so the priority was to try to have as much open space as possible. Since this is basically a basement, it was very important to find a way of getting natural light into every corner of the space. Thus, the two ends of the apartment (the doors to the terrace and the wall of the study) are made of glass. The colors and iconic pieces of furniture chosen complete a modern and vital space.

The perfect layout does not exist. Each family, each person, will have specific needs that will lead to a certain organization of space. In this case, the kitchen was situated in a passageway to give priority to the living room.

164

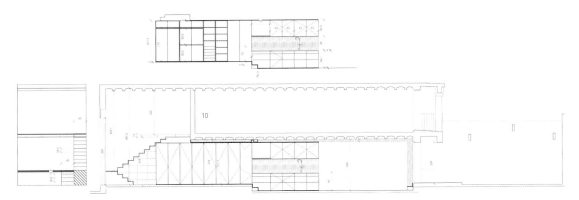

Sections

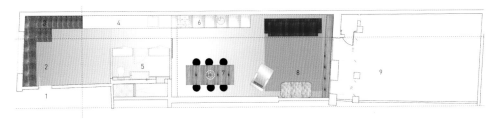

Floor plan

1. Entrance
2. Study
3. Staircase
4. Storage
5. Bathroom
6. Kitchen
7. Dining room
8. Living room
9. Terrace
10. Bedroom

165

The design of the staircase creates additional storage space, useful in the small spaces that combine living and work areas. The study area, located in the entrance hall, benefits from the light that enters through the translucent glass.

166

The bedroom was installed in a mezzanine built with simple metal beams and slats of wood that are left exposed. Unlike some mezzanines, the resulting height is comfortable with room for a normal bed.

HOME WORKSHOP
IN EL RAVAL

Architect: **Agustí Costa**
Location: **Barcelona, Spain**
Photos: **David Cardelús**
Square footage: **1,399 ft² (130 m²)**

The renovation of an apartment in El Raval district in Barcelona had to combine both work and living spaces. The initial criteria was very clear: the owner wanted three workshops, an IT area, storage space, and a living area with a kitchen, a dining room, a living room, a bedroom and a bathroom. The owner's deference to the architect as to what the renovation should entail was a major advantage for the architect, who could design an uninhibited project, where the relationship between the rooms would facilitate maximum visual interaction and the space would represent a contrast of original and modern design.

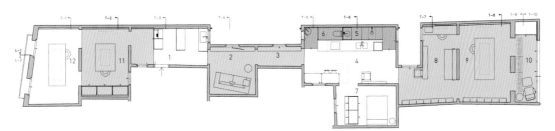

Floor plan before the renovation

Floor plan after the renovation

1. Entrance/storage
2. Living room
3. Corridor
4. Kitchen/dining room
5. Shower
6. Powder room
7. Bedroom
8. IT room
9. Workshop 1
10. Gallery
11. Workshop 2
12. Workshop 3

This renovation attempted to lighten the rooms and create spaces that flowed well. For this reason, as many walls as possible were torn down, obviously without compromising the structural stability.

167 The integration of original
elements into the new home is
illustrated in the mosaic floor,
which was restored with a
crystallized finish. The restoration
of the ceilings led to the recovery
of some of the plaster frames.

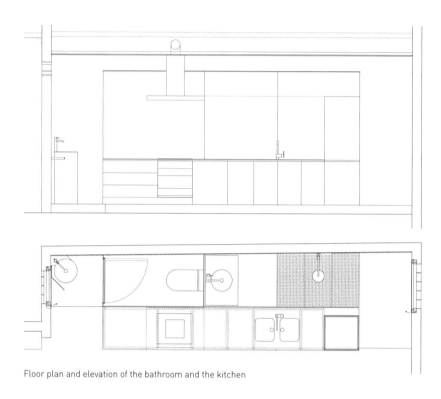

Floor plan and elevation of the bathroom and the kitchen

By moving the kitchen to the central area of the apartment, a long, narrow space was created. The bathroom is located in this area, and is divided into a shower area and a powder room in order to provide easy access to both areas.

168

The bathroom is tucked between walls of translucent glass. The semi-transparent glass and the color white provide diffused and indirect lighting that prevents any feeling of claustrophobia that such a narrow space may create.

Atelier KS © Atelier KS

Design Studios
© Bht Timmerman Photography

Mattias Laumayer/Paul McAneary Architects
McAneary Architects

171

Renovations seldom begin with a blank canvas for architects and interior designers. It is important to take into account the limitations in the use of materials and in the layout of the new spaces.

169

A good time to build an extension is when doing a renovation. If all the changes and renovations are carried out at the same time, you can save costs, time and the hassle associated with construction work.

170

Renovations increase the quality of life of the owners of an apartment, since interiors can be adapted to their lifestyle by improving the lighting and circulation, increasing storage space, etc.

172

If they are in good condition, retain original materials, such as wooden double doors and ceiling moldings, as they create an elegant contrast between the new and old.

173

It is advisable to retain some architectural elements when carrying out renovations, as they maintain the nobility of the original architecture even though they are combined with modern materials and designs.

175

Today, transforming an old industrial space into residential space is popular for its one main advantage: the spaces are open and allow for a flexible organization of the rooms, which can be adapted to each individual case.

176

You must ensure full compliance with all architectural heritage regulations for the apartment or home you want to renovate. If applicable, seek professional advice.

174

When renovating a home, extend it by using part of a flat roof or creating an attic area. You can gain space by taking advantage of a surface that was previously unused.

177

The purpose of renovation is to streamline and modernize the organization of spaces, so it is necessary to study the new layout in case you need to make the kitchen bigger, change the bathrooms or knock down partitions.

Paul Cha © Dao-Lou Zha

Nobbs Radford Architecture © Petter Bennets

179

Lifestyle changes drive changes in the use of homes. When renovating an apartment, redistribute the space and opt for the most favorable layout, such as joining the kitchen and the dining room.

Henning Stummel Architects © Luke Caulfield, Nigel Rigden

178

Renovation of an apartment should not overlook the need to change the facilities of the home, such as the pipes, the fittings, the wiring, or to improve insulation in doors or windows.

BUILDINGS

BISCORNET

Architect: **KOZ Architectes**
Location: **Paris, France**
Photos: **Sergio Grazia, Luc Boegly**
Square footage: **1,076–1,614 ft² (100–150 m²)**

Constructing a building on a lot in the Place de la Bastille is a challenge for any architect. The result is a building that fits into the environment like a glove. Maximum use has been made of the trapezoidal site, and the angles of the facades create spectacular effects, enhanced by the choice of materials: aluminum and glass slats. Metal panels, located on the side walls, create effects with the light and, when open, they reveal the colors of the facades. The glass slats of the main facade form a Venetian blind that changes the appearance of the building according to the opening angle.

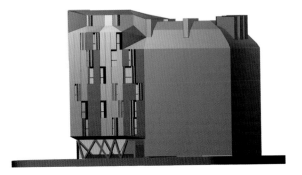
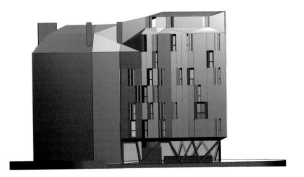
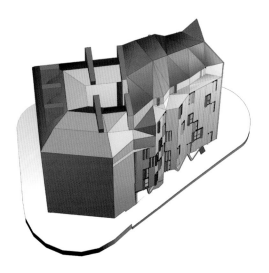
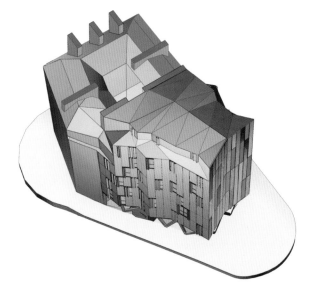

3-D representations

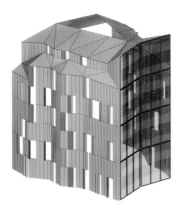

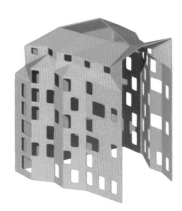

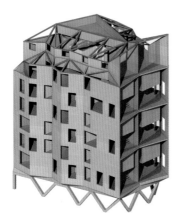

Axonometric diagram of the materials

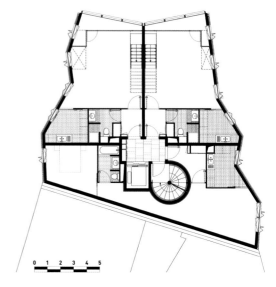

0 1 2 3 4 5

Level 1

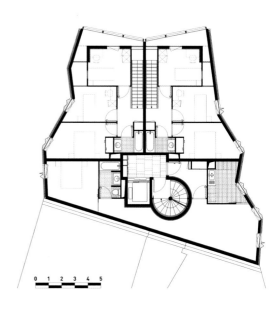

0 1 2 3 4 5

Level 2

The originality of the shape of the building
infiltrates into the interior. The top floor
apartments have high sloping ceilings that
create a unique and spacious zone.

Eight of the 14 apartments have semi-enclosed balconies that are formed in the space between the facade and the home. In addition to providing views, these balconies function as a second skin and help insulate the building and create air currents.

180 The use of glass in facades is increasing in office buildings, but it should not be dismissed as a solution in residential construction, as it provides additional insulation without losing visibility and light.

APARTMENTS IN CARABANCHEL

Architect: **Amann Cánovas Maruri**
Location: **Carabanchel, Spain**
Photos: **David Frutos**
Square footage: **645/796/958 ft² (60/74/89m²)**

This complex comprises 82 subsidized two, three or four bedroom apartments with a basement and an underground parking lot. All available space is capitalized on, including an open area in the center. Apartment buildings and urban life tend to hinder community life and small public spaces. To break this dynamic, the architects designed a central garden and openings in the homes to improve communication between private and public spaces, and to achieve more interaction. For example, the children who live in the complex can play together in the central garden.

Site plan

Axonometrics

181

The dynamism and communication that architects want to create among the residents of this building are also shown in the choice of the facade colors. Bright, cheerful colors are suitable for common spaces.

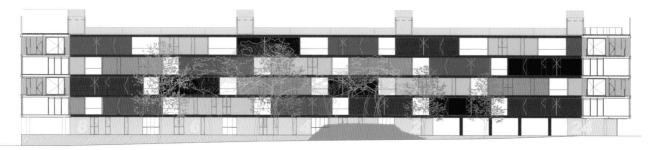

Section

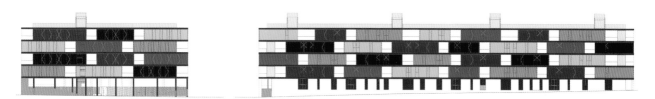

Elevations

Ground floor

Second-storey floor plan

In addition to the central space dedicated to the public garden, the architects included porches, courtyards and other building elements that create a social environmend that can be used year-round.

182

The construction of new buildings allows you to improve upon the design of older buildings. In the case of this project, the gaps on each floor allow ventilation throughout the building that improves thermal comfort.

COASTAL APARTMENTS

Architect: **OFIS Arhitekti**
Location: **Izola, Slovenia**
Photos: **Tomaz Gregoric**
Square footage: **322–1,130 ft² (30–105 m²)**

This project won a contest for the Housing Foundation of Slovenia, an organization that fosters the building of affordable housing for young families. The foundation's decision centered upon the flexibility of the floor plans, the economics of construction and the optimum use of the floor space. The location of the two five-storey buildings along the Adriatic led to the construction of balconies for every apartment, protected by colored awnings. The lack of structural elements in the interior of the apartments ensures the versatility of the spaces.

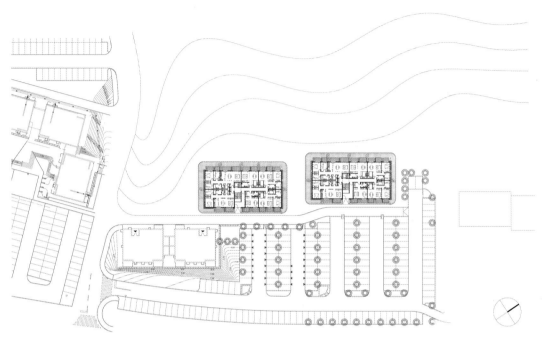

Site plan

The size of these apartments, 322 ft² (30 m²)
for the studios and 1,130 ft² (105 m²) for
the three-bedroom apartments, are small
compared to the standard in Slovenia.

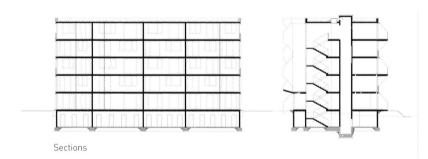

Sections

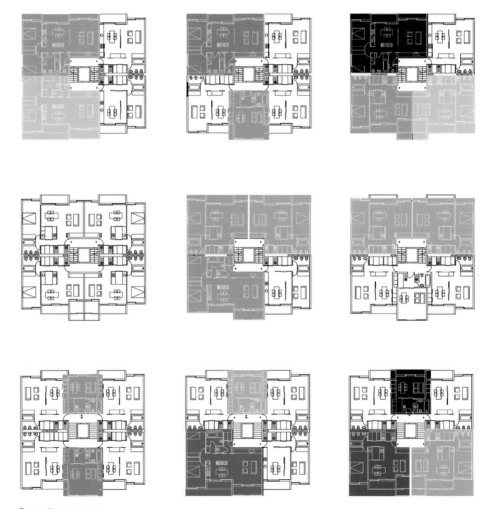

Types of apartments

183

It is advisable to include passive climate control systems. The structures that stick out from these facades occupy two floors, so that they contain the balcony from the upper floor and provide shade for the window of the lower floor.

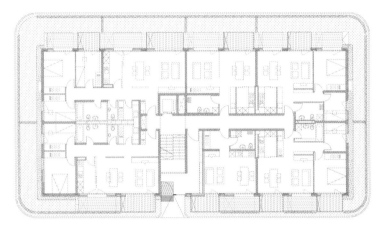

First floor

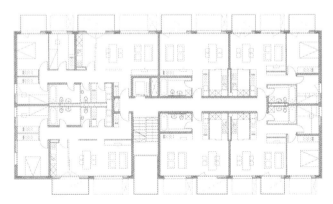

Second and fourth floors

184

It is possible to design a building that stands out and has an original style without being costly. The installation of different colored awnings is a practical and economical option to filter the light and create a unique atmosphere in the interiors.

CASAS 13 DE SEPTIEMBRE

Architect: **JSª Diseño Desarrollo**
Location: **Mexico City, Mexico**
Photos: **T. Casademunt, L. Gordoa, J. Navarrete**
Square footage: **645–1,291 ft² (60–120 m²)**

These 37 small apartments have been built in a former trade union warehouse. The renovation conserved the frame of the building, restoring and modifying it to create an empty space in which to erect the new homes. Partition walls were removed, and new roofs and facades were built. A notable feature is the central open courtyard, an original feature of the building that improves lighting in the apartments and that was maintained as a community space and as a place for neighbors to socialize. The apartments, all between 645 and 1,291 ft² (60 and 120 m²), have two levels and can be accessed through the courtyard.

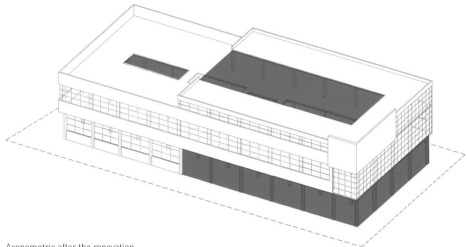

Axonometric after the renovation

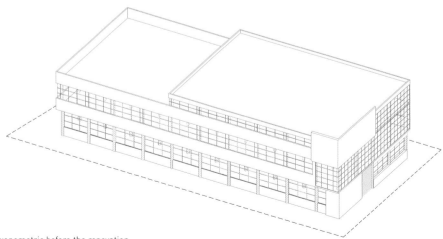

Axonometric before the renovation

The most used materials are steel in the metalworks and railings, aluminum for exterior siding, and wood for the walkways and the floors. The two longitudinal walkways are complemented by two cross walkways.

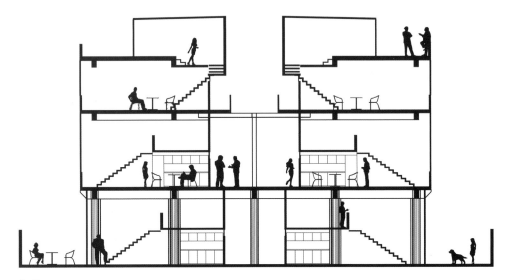

Section

Renovations have adapted the
layout of each apartment to
current needs, either in terms
of the distribution of the rooms
or the entry of light. This results
in a better quality of life for the
occupants.

185

MRG32

Architect: **LPzR Architetti Associati**
Location: **Milan, Italy**
Photos: **Chiara Pranzo-Zaccaria, Gabriele Pranzo-Zaccaria**
Square footage: **1,076 ft² (100 m²)**

This project involves the recovery of a building located within the interior of a courtyard for residential use. The existing one-floor building was a typical workshop from the 60s, with beams and concrete columns and a flat roof. The new construction has kept the original structure and shape and has remodeled the interior, which is now distributed among five homes with luxury finishes. Each unit has several interconnected levels. The presence of the glass increases the feeling of lightness and spaciousness. The bright red facade revitalizes the building.

Elevations

Renovation is typically more complex than
new construction. In this case, the structure
has been maintained and new elements have
been added, such as windows and blinds, that
have transformed the workshop into homes.

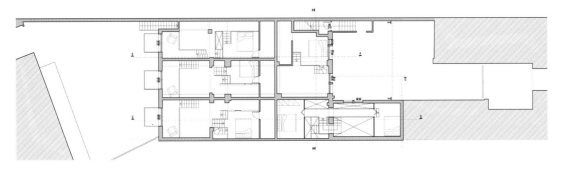

Basement

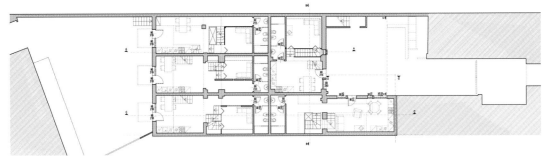

First floor

Second floor

186   The chosen materials (steel, glass and other more innovative materials, such as the Bencore Starlight polycarbonate panels) create bright spaces with a contemporary, minimalist aesthetic.

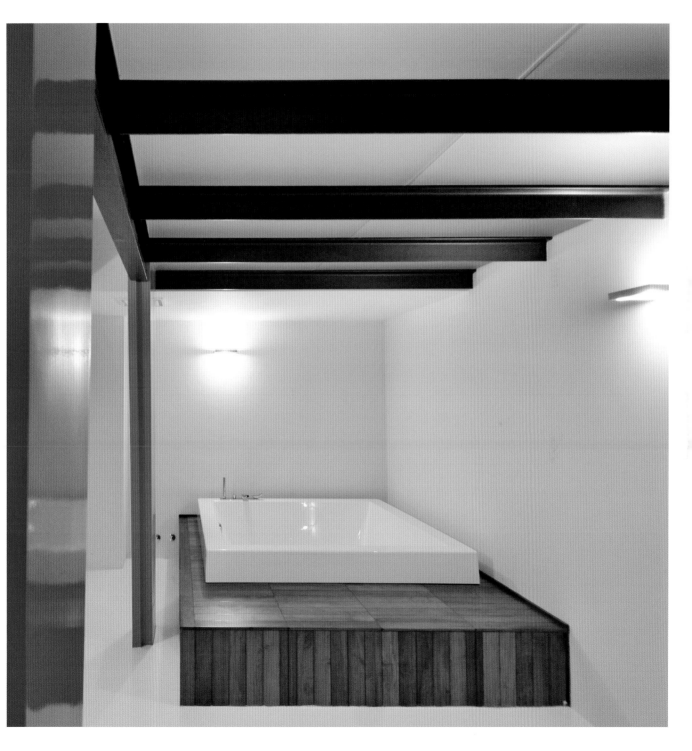

A7 LOFTS

Architect: **CMC Architects**
Location: **Prague, Czech Republic**
Photos: **Filip Slapal**
Square footage: **1,291–1,883 ft² (120–175 m²)**

The conversion of a former brewery into a residential complex, in which newly constructed buildings have also been erected, changes the visual landscape of the Holesovice district in Prague. In each building, spaces have been created that connect with the exterior: courtyards, balconies, atriums, terraces, etc. The different sizes and assorted layouts of the apartments seek to reflect the industrial architecture. For this reason, priority has been given to a loft and duplex type layout, with unified spaces and a bright ambience with a factory-style decor.

The kitchen and living room are a single space. This distribution is very common in more informal loft apartments. Open spaces are flexible, allowing them to easily change the use of a space.

Metal spiral staircases have
an industrial aesthetic.
Furthermore, this type of
staircase occupies less space,
they are easier to install and
require less infrastructure
and construction time.

187

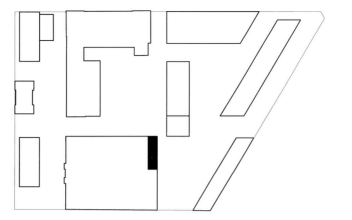

Site plan

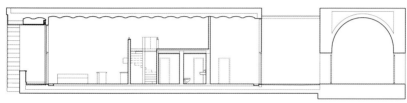

Section

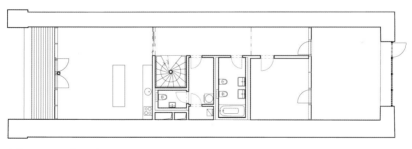

Loft apartment floor plan

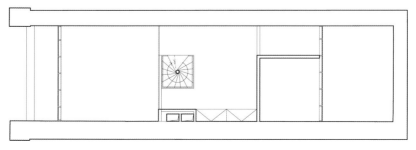

Mezzanine

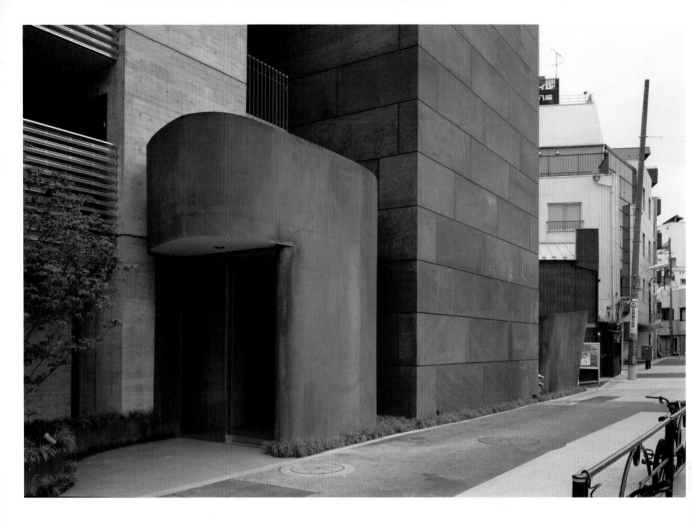

TOMIGAYA APARTMENTS

Architect: **Satoshi Okada**
Location: **Tokyo, Japan**
Photos: **Nacása & Partners**
Square footage: **538 ft² (50 m²)**

According to the architect Satoshi Okada, the growth of Tokyo over the past four decades has led to uncontrolled and improvised urbanization. In the lot where this building stands, an industrial area and a residential neighborhood converge. The designer of the building wanted to address the problem of the combination of traffic and residents without wasting the economic performance of the site. The solution was to reduce the visual impact by combining several structures of different heights and materials and by designing a **COR-TEN** steel structure that absorbs the overwhelming effect of the block.

The central tower, covered with rusty
galvanized steel plates, contains the elevator
and the fire escapes. The other two towers,
of different heights and coverings, are home
to 18 dwellings of seven different types.

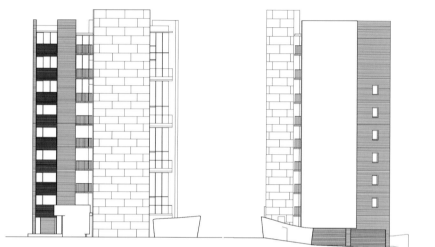

North and west elevations

South and east elevations

188 The steel structures, built with softer forms than the rest of the building, contain an access way to the complex and the space reserved resident storage.

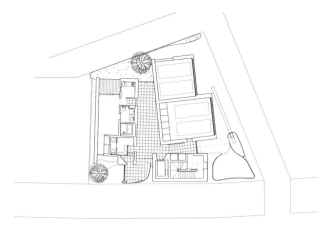

First floor

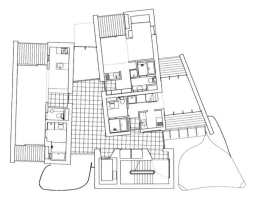

Second floor

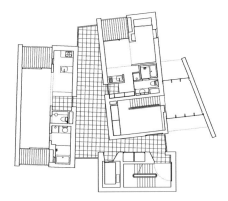

Third to fifth floor

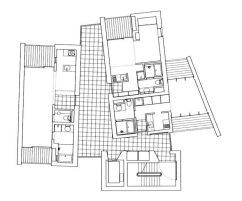

Sixth floor

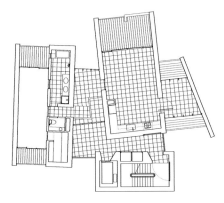

Eighth floor

Large buildings, which at times are built with cold materials, should include some spaces to a human scale and use careful lighting to mitigate the overwhelming effect of the height of the towers.

The interiors of the 538 ft^2 (50 m^2) homes combine
the color white with wooden floors and some
exposed concrete walls. This mixture of materials
accentuates the urban aspect of the apartments.

BUILDING IN YOYOGI PARK

Architect: **Yasui Hideo Atelier**
Location: **Tokyo, Japan**
Photos: **Nacas & Partners**
Square footage: **538 ft² (50 m²)**

This building is located in Yoyogi Park, next to one of the cities green lungs (a green space considered to be healthier because of its abundance of plantlife). It was decided that 14 dwellings spread over eight floors would be built on a 22 × 52 ft (7 × 16 m) site. The floor plan covers two apartments, located on either side of the core services. The kitchen and the bathrooms are located around the core services, while the living area and the bedroom occupy the opposite ends of the home. The apartments have a small balcony, protected from the neighbors by a metal strip. This layout ensures the lighting and the ventilation of the apartments, as they all are connected to the exterior.

Elevations

Narrow sites can be excellent for the construction of buildings, especially when located on wide streets or adjacent to parks or other open spaces. Any lighting and ventilation challenges can be surmounted with good design.

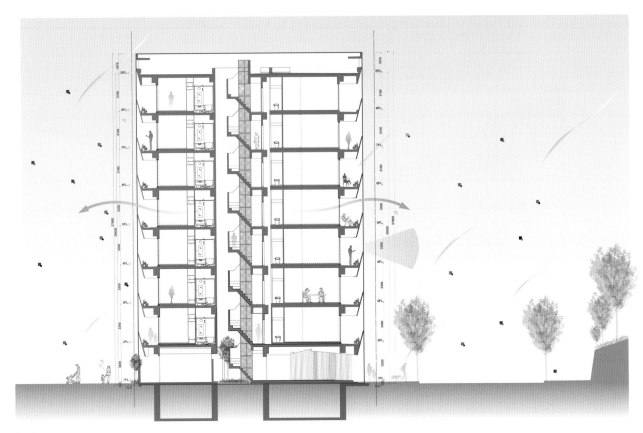

Section

The precise rectangular shape of the building,
along with openings in the east and west facades,
guarantee optimum cross ventilation, ideal for the
hot summers in Tokyo.

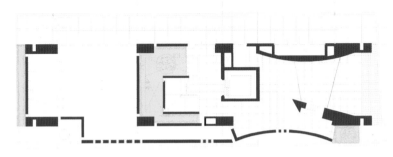

First floor

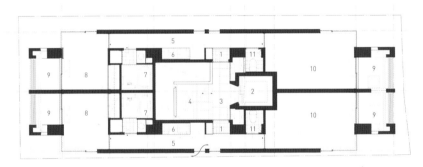

Floor plan

Given the limited area, the kitchen was
located along the corridor, which receives
abundant natural light through mullions
and two central openings. In the common
area, a long table serves as an office.

1. Entrance
2. Elevator
3. Landing
4. Staircase
5. Corridor
6. Kitchen
7. Bathroom
8. Bedroom
9. Balcony
10. Living room/dining room
11. Powder Room

A'CHRANNAG

Architect: **Gökay Deveci**
Location: **Rothesay, United Kingdom**
Photos: **Gökay Deveci, Andrew Lee**
Square footage: **484-914 ft² (45-85 m²)**

The architect was commissioned to build 14 subsidized homes that, besides being sustainable and innovative, also had local support. With that goal in mind, the community was given three choices: detached and semi-detached houses, low-rise buildings, or a circular tower. The tower was chosen because it took up less communal land and the homes would have good views. Each floor contains two apartments, one with two bedrooms and another with three bedrooms, both with south-facing balconies. The one-bedroom homes on the top level gave up some of their square footage to a circular terrace.

Sketch

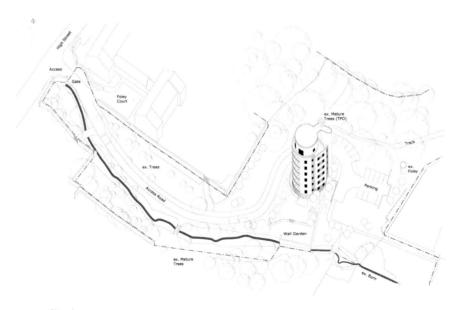

Site plan

189   In countries with colder climates and fewer hours of sunlight, balconies and terraces should be on the facade with the most sun exposure in order to enjoy these semi-open spaces for a longer time.

East and north elevations

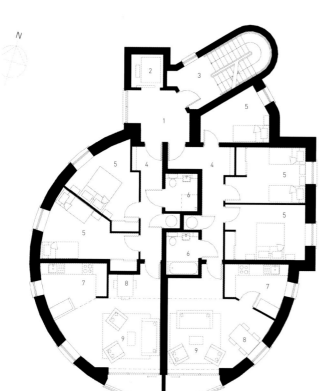

Floor plan

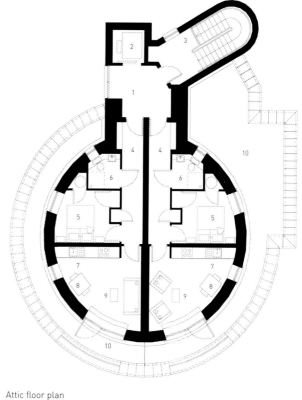

Attic floor plan

1. Landing
2. Elevator
3. Staircase
4. Entrance
5. Bedroom
6. Bathroom
7. Kitchen
8. Dining room
9. Living room
10. Terrace

The innovation of this building is in its original shape, the studied combination of materials and in the organic forms. These elements reduce the gap between public and private residential buildings common in Scotland.

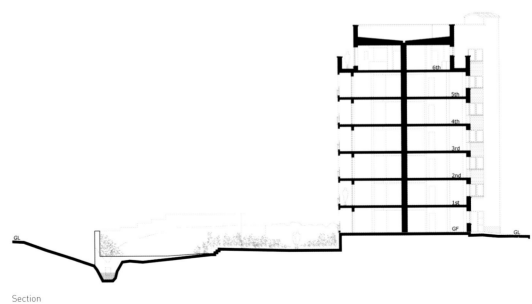

Section

On exteriors, simple and traditional materials applied to an original design can generate a distinctly contemporary building that contrasts with the prevailing architecture of the area.

LES NIDS

Architect: **Christophe Ouhayoun, Nicolas Ziesel/KOZ Architectes**
Location: **Courbevoie, France**
Photos: **Guillaume Grasset, JB Pellerin**
Square footage: **430–990 ft² (40–92 m²)**

The design of this subsidized housing was executed after reflecting on the meaning of family life and its relationship with architecture. A family home requires fast and fluid circulation and organization adapted to the changing needs of a family. The occupants must feel comfortable and at home, and they must also be able to establish relationships with neighbors. To these ends, the architects designed apartments with many windows and a lot of natural light, and with flexible layouts in private and common outdoor spaces that facilitate communication between neighbors.

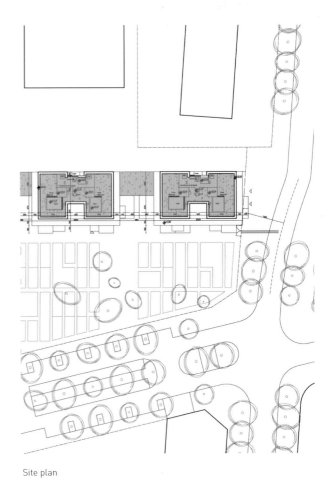

Site plan

The two buildings are divided into 28 dwellings.
This layout increased the surface area of the
facades, allowing more natural light into the
apartments and enhancing the views of Paris.

Level +1

Level +2

Level +3

Level +4

Level +5

Level +6

Level +7

The outdoor spaces extend the living areas of the apartments and facilitate communication with neighbors, building community links that are important in urban environments.

190

BUILDING MATERIALS

KOZ Architectes © Guillaume Grasset

192

Reinforced concrete is a great resource in the construction of apartment buildings. Its physical characteristics allow for the creation of countless forms, such as balconies and overhanging decks, or irregular sized floor plans.

KOZ Architectes / Sergio Grazia

191

Blinds are architectural elements that, in addition to their usefulness as protection against the sun and elements, can also contribute to the aesthetics of the apartment buildings because of the variety of existing forms and materials.

193

Metal is an inexpensive material that comes in many finishes, making it suitable for the exterior cladding of buildings. Paint and other treatments provide greater protection from the elements.

195

Textiles can be used on the exteriors of buildings. They are most commonly applied as awnings or blinds. It is the choice of fabric, color and shape that will define the aesthetics and the uniqueness of the building.

194

Metals, especially aluminum, are an excellent material for exterior work. Its lightweight structure and strength allow you to create complex frames on which to assemble blinds, slats of other materials, etc.

197

Glass is a material often used in the facades of office buildings. The reasons behind its use, better insulation and visibility, can also be applied to residential constructions.

196

For exterior design, consider using materials that were traditionally non-resistant to weathering. Wood, if it has received a protective treatment, can be used for walkways inside the building and create contrast with other materials.

JSª Diseño Desarrollo © T. Cardelemunt, L. Gordoa, J. Navarrete

199

Security features are extremely important in buildings and must follow strict regulations. It is common to use metal and safety glass for access railings and balconies.

KOZ Architectes © JB Pellerin

198

Satoshi Okada © Nacása & Partners

It is important to design for ease of access for pedestrians and vehicles if there is a parking lot, because it facilitates the entry and exit of the residents. Materials must be strong enough to support the weight of people and vehicles.

Amann Cánovas Maruri © Miguel de Guzmán

200

Whenever possible, apartment buildings should have covered outdoor areas done in materials that allow for proper air ventilation as well as protection from the rain so that people can walk around in comfort.

CONTRIBUTOR DIRECTORY

.27 Architects
Thessaloniki, Greece
www.point27.gr

Agustí Costa
Berga, Spain
www.agusticosta.com

Amann Cánovas Maruri
Madrid, Spain
www.amann-canovas-maruri.es

Apollo Architects & Associates
Tokyo, Japan
www.kurosakisatoshi.com

Atmos Studio
London, United Kingdom
www.atmosstudio.com

Barbara Appolloni
Barcelona, Spain
www.barbaraappolloni.com

Bárbara Aurell
Barcelona, Spain
www.espacioenblancoestudio.com

Carola Vannini Architecture
Rome, Italy
www.carolavannini.com

Centrala
Warsaw, Poland
www.centrala.net.pl

CHRYSTALLINE Architect
Jakarta, Indonesia
www.chrystallineartchitect.com

CJ Studio
Taipei, Taiwan
www.shi-chieh-lu.com

CMC Architects
Prague, Czech Republic
www.cmc-architects.cz

Craig Steely Architecture
San Francisco, CA, USA
http://craigsteely.com

Data AE
Barcelona, Spain
www.dataae.com

DEDENTRO
Boadilla del Monte, Spain
www.dedentro.com

Edwards Moore
Melbourne, Australia
http://edwardsmoore.com

Entre 4 Parets
Barcelona, Spain
www.entre4parets.com

Fabrica 718
New York, NY, USA
www.fabrica718.com

FORMA Design
Washington DC, USA
www.formaonline.com

Frédéric Flanquart
Paris, France
www.frederic-flanquart.com

Gökay Deveci
Aberdeen, United Kingdom
g.deveci@rgu.ac.uk

GRAFT Gesellschaft von Architekten
Berlin, Germany
www.graftlab.com

Héctor Ruiz Velázquez
Madrid, Spain
www.ruizvelazquez.com

Hideki Yoshimatsu/Archipro Architects
Tokyo, Japan
www.archipro.net

i29 | interior architects
Duivendrecht, The Netherlands
www.i29.nl

Ian Ayers, Francesc Zamora
Barcelona, Spain
ianayers@gmail.com

Íñigo Beguiristáin
Pamplona, Spain
i.beguiristain@coavn.org

Jeff Etelamaki Design Studio
New York, NY, USA
www.je-designstudio.com

JSª Diseño Desarrollo
Mexico DF. Mexico
www.jsa.com.mx

Kelly Reynolds Interiors
Vancouver, BC Canada
www.kellyreynoldsinteriors.com

Kimberly + John Canale
New York, NY, USA
www.inspiredgoodness.com

KOZ Architectes
Paris, France
www.koz.fr

Leone Design Studio
New York, NY, USA
www.leonedesignstudio.com

LKMK Architects
Vrilissia, Greece
www.lkmk.gr

LPzR Architetti Associati
Milan, Italy
www.lpzr.it

MAAJ Architectes
Paris, France
www.maaj.fr

Michele Gambato Architetto
Pádova, Italy
www.mgark.it

Michelle Mason
London, United Kingdom
www.michellemason.co.uk

mihadesign
Tokyo, Japan
http://mihadesign.com

Mis Mas
Barcelona, Spain
www.mis-mas.com

Mplusm architects
Athens, Greece
www.mplusm.gr

Nacho Polo Interior Designer
Madrid, Spain
www.nachopolo.com

Nest Architects
Melbourne, VIC, Australia
www.nestarchitects.com.au

Norm Architects
Copenhagen, Denmark
www.normcph.com

OFIS Arhitekti
Ljubljana, Slovenia
www.ofis.si

Oneto/Sousa Arquitectura Interior
Lima, Peru
www.onetosousa.com

Parasite Studio
Timisoara, Romania
www.parasitestudio.com

Paul Coudamy
Paris, France
http://paulcoudamy.com

Pekka Littow Architectes
Boulogne-Billancourt, France
www.littowarchitectes.com

Pensando en Blanco
Guipúzcoa, Girona, Spain
www.pensandoenblanco.com

Plystudio
Singapore, Singapore
www.ply-studio.com

Ptang Studio
Hong Kong, China
www.ptangstudio.com

Pugh & Scarpa
www.pugh-scarpa.com

Satoshi Okada
Tokyo, Japan
www.okada-archi.com

sciskewcollaborative
New York, NY, USA
Shangai, China
Singapore, Singapore
www.sciskew.com

S.DREI Architektur
Graz, Austria
www.sdrei.com

SPaN (Stonely Pelsinski Architects Neukomm)
New York, NY, USA
www.span-ny.com

Tad & Jessica Carpenter
Kansas City, KS, USA
http://tadcarpenter.com

Tang Kawasaki Studio
New York, NY, USA
www.tangkawasaki.com

Ten to One Design Building
New York, NY, USA
www.tenonedesignbuild.com

Vora Arquitectura
Barcelona, Spain
www.vora-arquitectura.com

VSA concept
Brussels, Belgium
www.wix.com/vsaconcept/vsaconcept

Yasui Hideo Atelier
Tokyo, Japan
www.yasui-atr.com

YLAB Arquitectos
Barcelona, Spain
www.ylab.es

Zottl Buda
Vienna, Austria
www.zottlbuda.at